FROM COTTON FIELDS TO MEDICINE

An autobiography

by HAZEL COLEY-GREENE, M. D.

Copyright @2020 by Hazel Coley-Greene

All rights reserved. No part of this book may be reproduced in any form or by any electronic or mechanical means, including information storage and retrieval systems, without permission in writing from the publisher, except by reviewers, who may quote brief passages in a review.

This publication contains the opinions and ideas of its author. It is intended to provide helpful and informative material on the subjects addressed in the publication. The author and publisher specifically disclaim all responsibility for any liability, loss or risk, personal or otherwise, which is incurred as a consequence, directly or indirectly, of the use and application of any of the contents of this book.

WORKBOOK PRESS LLC
187 E Warm Springs Rd,
Suite B285, Las Vegas, NV 89119, USA

Website:	https://workbookpress.com/
Hotline:	1-888-818-4856
Email:	admin@workbookpress.com

Ordering Information:
Quantity sales. Special discounts are available on quantity purchases by corporations, associations, and others.
For details, contact the publisher at the address above.

ISBN-13:   978-1-953839-41-1 (Paperback Version)
           978-1-953839-42-8 (Digital Version)

REV. DATE: 24/09/2020

Contents

Foreword 8

Chapter One Early Childhood 9

Chapter Two School Days 23

Chapter Three Leaving Childhood 40

Chapter Four The Tide Turns 49

Chapter Five The Doctoral Years 66

Chapter Six The Beginning of the End 82

Chapter Seven A Dream Realized 94

Epilogue 104

*This book is dedicated to
my cousin NANCY
who took time out from her busy life
to comfort my heart.*

THANK YOU

To the DUNAMS Family-
Whose concern helped me through the trying time.

To SELENA
Whose friendship helped me through the crying time.

To PAT PATTERSON-
Whose presence helped me through the darkest time.

To GOD-
Who is there for me all the time.

SPECIAL THANKS

To Phoenix, my only child, for comfort, trust and faith.

To Sherri, my heart of Gold, for unmeasurable fidelity.

-L. Coley-Greene-

Foreword

At the age of forty-four, my mother set out to accomplish what no other American woman of color had achieved at her age—to graduate and receive a Doctorate of Medicine and Surgery from the Université Libre de Bruxelles, Belgium.

She walked two and a half miles daily from the cotton fields to a one-room school that housed grades one through seven taught by one teacher. But it was her thirst for knowledge that would sustain her and carry her to a great adventure across the Atlantic.

We hope that the content of these pages will inspire many other young persons to strive and become whatever they wish to become, overcoming any obstacles and defying all odds.

Autobiographies provide insight into the past, present, and future, as they are passed from generation to generation.

They contribute to the family fiber.
They can also assist in establishing one's self-worth, and identity for ages to come, thus meshing a sense of belonging and family heritage.

Lillie Coley-Greene

Hazel Coley-Greene

Chapter One
Early Childhood

I am a product of the fifth conception of my parents—a long awaited female, especially by my father, since there were already five males including a multiple birth. I was born April 7, 1908, in the township of Saulston, North Carolina. The unusual circumstance about my birth was that I was the first girl. I was born in a house which was formerly occupied by the owner of the plantation who had migrated to the nearby city of Goldsboro.

My mother was a beautiful, dashing country girl with long black hair who married my father in 1898 at the age of twenty-one. Her name was Lillie Isabel Lewis. She was a native of Selma, North Carolina, and her parents were tenant farmers—a skill learned directly from her grandmother's people, Cherokee Indians who settled in that region. It was from them that she learned the art of being a very efficient housewife and helpmate to her husband, who had acquired the knowledge of a proficient farmer.

Her parents were Hack Lewis and Clara Etta Shirrod and together they had two daughters and five sons and they both lived until each child was grown, which is desirable in the life of all parents.

The first daughter was named Nancy Lewis and she married a Hawkins. She and her four brothers chose to be city dwellers while my mother and her brother, Joseph Berry Lewis, remained on the farm. My Uncle Needham and Uncle Willie Hack Lewis pursued apprentices as brick masons and house constructors in Raleigh, Goldsboro, and several other cities in North Carolina—which was an outstanding achievement and today some of their works are still standing.

My Uncle James Leonard was a fireman in Norfolk, Virginia, and finally in Roxbury and Milton, Massachusetts, where he reared his family of two daughters and one son. His wife was named Blanche Hankins Lewis. My Uncle Barney migrated to Buffalo, New York, followed the trade of cabinetmaker, and had one son who became a successful carpenter as well.

My Uncle William Hack, whom I mentioned, fathered two sons who followed his trade and two daughters who were teachers. Uncle Needham, the other brick mason, was married to Hattie Wooten but had no children, so he took an active interest in the females born to his sister and brothers by attempting to send them to school. Since I was the eldest of the females born in the family on my mother's side, I was the first one to receive financial assistance toward a higher education. When contacted, I had graduated from high school, which was in 1928, and he wanted me to go to college instead of nurse's training which I was about to pursue. He stated that he wanted me to go to college because he wanted me to be a "Great Woman." Going to college to him was a great achievement and subconsciously, that idea stuck with me and during my struggle, when the going would get rough, "I want you to be a great woman" would serve as a booster to my endeavor.

Another idea which also gave me courage when I needed it came from my Aunt Nancy. We were riding with our family doctor one night and out of the blue she said, "You know, she might read medicine someday." There was nothing in her conversation at the time that prompted her to make such a statement, but the thought of it boosted me whenever I needed to be.

My mother's people on a whole were considered aggressive in spite of their lack of formal education. My mother was born in 1876 and attended the one-room school in the vicinity for about three months out of the year for several years. She was able to read, write, and understand basic arithmetic. She was interested in the domestic aspect of homemaking and at an early age learned how to cook and sew—skills she learned from her grandmother. So when it became necessary to be out in public life, she and her sister, Nancy were able to make their own clothes, which was a credit to the family and was admired by the whole community. She did not have a job outside of the family circle so she spent a great deal of time assisting her mother with the younger children; and because she was very proud and beautiful, she had no trouble attracting the opposite sex; and when the gentlemen would see her going by, they would stand at attention until she was well out of sight. Then they would make complimentary remarks about the way she carried herself and her personal appearance. She was considered the most beautiful girl in the township and she was almost at this stage of development when she met my father.

My father was named James Ervin Coley. His parents were Rachael Exum and Peter Coley, who was a direct descendant of the slave master Coley line. I remember that there were three sons and eight daughters and almost all of them had several children of their own. They were all tenant farmers and many of the children followed the same occupation and there was no special skills exhibited or family customs manifested. He was born on January 10, 1864, in the township of Stantonburg, North Carolina, Wilson County. He grew up in that vicinity but later migrated to Boston, Massachusetts, with his cousin who finally settled there. During his stay he was employed by the Stanford Memorial Hotel as a waiter and he thought seriously of remaining in Boston until he was bereaved by the death of one of his sisters and was unable to attend the funeral. So he vowed that he would never be so far away that he could not be present on another such occasion. When he was asked why he did not return to Boston after he had married, he remarked several times that he would rather be a king in his own province than be an underdog in the big city. All in all, I don't think his desire was to be so far removed from his family. During his early childhood, he remained with the family and assisted in rearing the younger children since he was the eldest son; but as he approached manhood, he would hire himself out to other farmers in his community. He did not show or manifest any special skill, but whatever he did, he did it well and he developed the art of an efficient farmer.

His schooling was sparse. His school was a one-room shack, but he often referred to his teacher, Mr. John Skinner, who was responsible for his meager book training and his ardor for reading in which he developed a great skill. In his middle years, during World War I, he was the center of attraction of his neighbors by describing the war as though he was on the front line. He bought books of all the wars, as much as he could obtain, and spoke intelligently about each one of them. His knowledge along those lines were phenomenal.

Pop taking a rest on the farm circa, 1911

Hazel Coley-Greene

During the early 1900s, the horse and buggy and the horse and wagon were the vogue especially for the poor and black. For amusement, the people of the many rural areas enjoyed picnics, ball games, set dancing, etc., especially by Saturday when the week's work had come to an end. One beautiful Saturday afternoon, while the guests were enjoying their feasting of the goodies that had been prepared for the occasion, a young man suddenly spied a young woman and became deeply infatuated. He said, "Great, Scotts, who is that beautiful gal with the big eyes that I see near the grandstand?" He was told by one of his friends that she was Miss Lillie Isabel Lewis, old man Hack Lewis' daughter. In the meantime, she had made an equally interesting discovery and upon inquiring had been told that he was Mr. James E. Coley—who had recently returned from Boston where he had been spending some time with his cousin. They were introduced and the courtship began immediately.

After a few months, my father and mother decided to marry. My grandfather was informed that my father was coming over to ask for my mother's hand and he was so overwhelmed that he snatched a pillow and crawled under the bed and was asleep when my father arrived. He was awakened and the mission was completed that day and they were married in 1898.

My parents set up housekeeping in a small two-room farmhouse in the field on the farm of Mr. George Rackley. They worked very well together from the start for the good of the entire unit, but she worked in the fields as well as in the home. It was not long before she was expecting their first child. She named him James Arthur. He was not a well child and did not live longer than one and a half years. A year later, her second child came named George Emmett; and one and a half years later, twins were born in the family-named Freeman and Leeman. By this time the family had moved into the former family home of the landlord, who had moved to the city of Goldsboro, North Carolina. He and my mother had become close friends. He had recently lost his wife so he would come out to the farm and turn to my mother for solace and comfort in his time of bereavement. She would prepare a place for him to relax and prepare nice meals for him. Fried chicken would almost always be on the menu and other goodies such as hot buttermilk biscuits and potato pie. This went on several months until he became stronger and more independent.

In the meantime, the family was blessed with the arrival of another son. He was named Needham Edmond Coley. This was the fourth in the series of births and my father began to wonder how long he was going to be the father of sons without the arrival of a daughter. My mother was contented to have all boys because she felt that they had a better chance to make it in the world than females, so she went on her merry way. This was the fifth son and she was happy. About two years later, on April 7, 1908, the tide turned. Instead of a bouncing boy, a female child was born. My mother was happy to have a healthy child, but my father was overjoyed to have a little girl to cuddle. I was named Ethelene Coley after one of my mother's best friends; but when I was in junior high school, Hazel was added to Ethelene by one of my best friends, Mrs. Alfreda Hill Carey. This change was done and accepted by the Bureau of Vital Statistics. Since I was a girl, Mother appeared to get a great joy in caring for me in my early childhood. Instead of continuing to make suits for her four boys, some of the time was spent in making clothes for me, especially little dresses, which she drafted without a commercial pattern and soon she began to realize that I could be an important entity in her life. My father felt that my presence was the beginning of a balance of nature. His attention was divided between me and the boys. The boys, too, were proud of their little sister, but there appeared to be a sibling bond between Freeman and the baby and he became the babysitter. My mother could trust him with me better than she could the rest of the boys. One day, Leeman, the twin to Freeman, was playing in the yard and he saw a large worm. He called out, "Freeman! Freeman! Come and see the worm, come and see the worm." Freeman replied, "No, the baby will fall. You come and stay with the baby and let me see the worm." Leeman answered, "Let the baby fall if she wants to and you come and see the worm." By this time, my mother returned and arrested what might have been a disaster.

*Our family on the farm—Wayne County, N.C., 1910
left to right cousin Bobby, cousin Jonnet, Edmond,
Freeman and Leeman (twins)
Emmett, Pop, Mama (Poke in arms) Ethelene and cousin Essie*

While my mother was getting fully adjusted to me as the first female, exactly one and a half years later, a second girl was born on September 15, 1910. She was given the name Pocahontas, an Indian name, after one of her friends. She appeared to be more alert than I was and won the favor of many members of the family, especially her brothers and uncles on my mother's side. She could follow instructions from my mother and do just as well or better than she was taught. She talked at an earlier age than I did and when one of our uncles told her that she cries when she gets her hair combed, she said, "you're a lie, I am not." That was amusing to my uncle, but my mother would correct her as she saw fit.

When she was seven years old, she picked 107 pounds of cotton. When she was thirteen, she picked 390 pounds; but I could never get beyond 197 pounds. My attention and training were more domestic and centered around the home. When she was two years old, another boy was born into the family. He was named William Earl Coley, but he became ill and he died before he was a year old. Mother was saddened at the loss of her baby. I remember how sad she looked at the burial. He was born a normal, healthy child and remained so for several months. The exact nature of the illness that caused his death I don't recall. The birth of another child soon followed, but he too became ill and he died before his first birthday. The cause of death was spinal meningitis. He was named Ronnie Lee Coley. This was the second blow in so short a span of time. Many months passed before my mother overcame the catastrophe. I feel that the birth of another child which soon followed did a great deal in healing the breach that was caused by the two successive deaths.

On July 27, 1914, a male child was born. He had my mother's big, bright eyes and he was named Ronald Merron Coley. A very special bond was formed between him and my mother very early in his life that lasted well into his adulthood. Exactly eleven months later to the day, my mother's last child was born on June 27, 1915, and although my mother was ill at the time, the baby survived the birth and was a healthy girl. She was named Clara Etta Coley. That was my grandmother's name and she grew to be a healthy woman and managed to maintain herself and make a good living in her lifetime. In her early womanhood, she spent a great deal of time caring for our aging mother, but I became the caregiver in 1950 until I left for Europe.

In summary, my mother bore eight sons and three daughters, making eleven children in all with ten conceptions. Out of the eleven children born, eight lived to adulthood, three daughters including me, and five boys.

There are many events that take place during one's early childhood. The first that I am able to recall is the burial of one of my mother's babies who had died. Family and friends went by horse and buggy or by wagon. I went seated in the front of the buggy of a friend on a little stool. My younger sister Pocahontas was in the front of the buggy that carried my parents. I wanted so much to ride with them but there was not enough room and the homely faces of these two old ladies with whom I was riding remained in my mind for many months. The weeping of my mother at the grave site was hard to erase from my memory. The house was still, sad, and somber for many weeks but finally, everything began to fall back into business as usual.

In my day and in the rural district, emphasis was placed on toys only at a special time, and that time was Christmas. My parents made an effort for each child to receive a toy from Santa Claus. My mother used that as an incentive for us to work at our chores around the home and in the fields. My brothers would receive a toy they chose for boys such as trains, trucks, and carved animals while they were small. As they grew older, they chose their own such as firecrackers and cap guns. From time to time, someone would get shot in the hand or on the leg, sustaining a minor injury that had to be dealt with. One of the brothers manipulated his cap pistol and it went off in my face. I was more frightened than injured. The scream excited my father so my brother got a flogging. My mother got angry at me for causing the whole incident.

The toys for the girls consisted of dolls, dishes, and tea sets, but she did not concentrate on dolls very much. I personally loved dolls and I talked almost half a year, saying that I hoped Santa would bring me a doll. When the morning arrived, I saw a box about the size of a doll about a foot in length. When I investigated, I found it to be a pin cushion, one for me and one for my sister who did not seem to mind at all—but I did. I cried secretly for many weeks because I did not get this doll that I wanted so desperately from Santa Claus. Dolls were my favorite toys but I was not favored with many of them. My most beautiful one was given to me by Aunt Nancy when I was in a doll drill at school. She was the most beautiful doll in the drill and the best dressed. My mother dressed her in one of my baby sister's dresses. Many of the other girls had rag dolls that their mothers had made. My mother did not want me to play with her when she was not around from fear that I might break her and surely enough, I was playing with her one day when she was out and my father called for water while he was plowing in the field. I left my doll and took the water to him and when I returned, I found her face down with her head broken. I felt that a member of the family had been fatally injured. That is the one time I wished I had listened to my mother. Some years later, my cousin gave me her doll which she had

had for a long time. She was old and did not last very long and her eyes soon fell out. I managed to get another doll which I ordered from a company. I liked her though she was inexpensive, but my mother gave her to my cousin to play with and when the little girl saw the eyes open and close, she became frightened and threw it on the floor and broke her head. As well as I can recall that was the last doll for me. I cannot remember having received another from my mother, which I was never able to understand. I wonder if it was because of that uncontrollable dislike or lack of interest or the female rivalry that has been known to exist between mothers and daughters. Very often I felt left out and it would manifest itself by my crying. Perhaps I was oversensitive but my brothers and some other members of my family would show preference to my sister. By some I was given the nickname of "Lard" because I was fat and did not take to dressing very well. My feet were disproportionate to my size, so one of my nicknames was "Big Foot." I was ashamed of my feet until I was married and suffered all through high school and college days with painful feet. When my husband found this out, he said, "You should get a shoe that fits regardless of the size. You did not make your feet and there is no need to be ashamed of them." From that day on, I could buy shoes with the pleasure of knowing that they would not hurt my feet and as I grew older, my sensitivity was greatly diminished and I learned to face obstacles and rejections which I was destined to meet in later life.

Nursery rhymes and bedtime stories were not a great part of my early childhood; however, I was acquainted with a few of them such as Hickory Dickory Dock, To Market To Market, The Three Little Pigs, The Three Bears, and Little Sally Walker. After the days' work was done, my family was worn from struggling dawn to dusk and the evening time was spent in the preparation and eating of the evening meal and the night chores. My mother would sew and make quilts so we could be warm at night and my father would busy himself reading the newspaper which he received daily. It was a generation later when I was hired out as a nursemaid that I became familiar with the idea of reciting nursery rhymes and bedtime stories. Our recreation for the evening consisted of playing Hide and Go Seek and watching bats chase insects for food in the wide open barnyard.

There were no trees in it; thus it offered plenty of room for frolicking, especially on moonlit nights. The front yard was filled with maple and cedar trees and we spent a great deal of time catching fireflies at night when they were in season.

The Rackley homestead contained many fruit trees of various kinds: cherry, plum, fig, pear, peach, apple, and grapevines. When the rains came and we could not work in the fields, we would be obligated to can the fruits for the winter. My family owned several cows and when one was expecting a young one, we would try to stay awake at night to see the delivery take place; but we were never successful. It would always happen during the day when our parents were around and so we only got to see the finished product, the young calf.

There were many events that I can remember from my preschool days, some of those that are outstanding, so I will relate a few. I have often referred to my sister who was younger than I but had a greater ability of self-comportment. When she took a notion to, she would give me a flogging at will, being encouraged by my brothers, but one day I mustered enough courage to fight back and I won the bout. After that time, the tide turned and I had no fear of a beating from her.

Another event that was outstanding was our trip to the County Fair of 1917 in Goldsboro, North Carolina. My mother and Uncle Joseph, her brother, set out early one morning with six members of their family in a two-horse wagon. The children were seated on the floor of the wagon on quilts to cushion the blows by the shocks of the wheels and we suffered soreness of the abdominal muscles for more than a week after it was over, despite the quilts for shock absorbers. It was a very enjoyable day and a new discovery of city lights, the first ride on a trolley car, the strong smell of the train smoke, and the introduction of Cracker Jacks, hot dog, horse racing, and many animals in action. When I am attending a circus now, I am well reminded of that first day with the fair and the joy of eating my fill of my first hot dogs and sweet popcorn.

The preparation for this trip was a big job for my mother. She combed the girls' hair and had us all take a bath the night before. She prepared a dinner of fried chicken, cake, and biscuits for the day at the fair because it would have cost much money to feed the eight of us. Mr. Rackley, our landlord, permitted us to leave the wagon and mules at his place for the day, so there Mother would feed us before going to the fairgrounds. The trolley ride was so exciting. I can see my mother and uncle now getting us all on and off the trolley. The event remained in my mind for a long, long time.

About two years later, the financial status of the family improved. The farm products were bringing in a better profit. We were able to purchase a phonograph and an automobile which would seat every member of the family. My father bought an insurance policy for the protection of the family in the event of his death and he also bought a farm of our own. But the financial odds went against him in a short period of time and there was a loss of almost 143 acres of land. But we enjoyed the use of our new car for many years, especially since it would accommodate the entire family in an emergency.

Our farm was not as serviceable as it might have been. We did not have ample space for farming and we had to rent from other farmers to complete our crops. That necessitated the cleaning of new ground by my brothers which robbed them of their chance of spending more time in school and the fall in the price of farm products brought about a curtailment of spending, so the older brothers sought work in the city to help carry the financial load.

We had relatives who lived across the field on their own farm—my aunt Emily and she was very fond of her niece's children and when my mother was ill, she would care for us. She would comb and braid our hair and give us a bath when it was necessary. She would always have candy to give to us when we were around and she was always showing us off to her friends.

When I was small, my favorite food was ham. My mother said that she had a recollection of me getting choked on a piece when she was in bed and could not reach me. She said she cried out for help and someone came and plucked the ham from my throat and she was so relieved. When I was about five years old, my mother started teaching me how to do small chores and among the first were sitting with the baby, sweeping, keeping the chickens off the porch, and drying the dishes.

The first holiday that I can remember was Thanksgiving. There would be a large turkey, several chickens, pumpkin and potato pies, cakes, and a barbequed pig. My father would roast it over an open pit in the yard and the feast would be in the middle of the day. I remember one Thanksgiving day, our money was short and a white neighbor, Mr. Ernest Smith, contracted us to pick cotton for him that day. All the children were sad because we had to work and all the other children were able to go to church and visit their friends and enjoy the entire day as a holiday. The day spent in the cotton field was a profit financially because the money was needed for winter clothes.

The church we were affiliated with was a village church where the people gathered for programs. My parents were of a different denomination, the Primitive Baptist faith. There were no children connected with it, no evening services, and no programs and the blacks and whites used the same building but the blacks sat behind the minister and entered through the backdoor. When the quarterly meetings were held, many people who were members of the same faith would come from miles around on their horses and buggies for the services. One of our houses would be the meeting place for singing and praying and there would be feasting for two days on the goodies that my mother had prepared.

The Christmas holidays were well celebrated by my family. We would spend a week of feasting and visiting friends and relatives. In addition, there would be the preparation of the turkey, chickens, a goose, a pig or pork roast, and many cakes and pies, and the baskets filled with apples, oranges, nuts, grapes, coconuts, candies, and raisins. There would be enough food and fruits to share with visitors and friends.

I recall at one time that a convict camp was pitched near our home. It was made up of black and white workers and on a Christmas day, my mother, with the help of the family, prepared chicken dinner for the whole camp including the officers. It consisted of huge pots of chicken and chicken stew, a kind of pastry like a dumpling, and huge pans of potato pudding, and many vegetables and fruits. The prisoners and the personnel were overjoyed at such a gesture of kindness from a family in the neighborhood; and the family was equally as happy to have done such a kindness. We were highly praised by all the people of the vicinity and my mother was especially touched because she had a friend who had a son who was one of the prisoners in the group.

The house that I lived in was the largest one on the plantation. It was the former home of the landlord and there were four additional houses on the land, two of which were demolished some years earlier because they had lost their usefulness. Our house was actually too small for our growing family. At one time, there were six or seven males, three females, and my parents—making a total of eleven persons at one time in a four-room house with two porches and a hallway. Our source of heat was two fireplaces that everyone sat around trying to keep warm on cold winter nights. There was a room called the boys' room and Mama and Papa's room housing them, the females, and the baby. There was almost always a quilt rack strung from the ceiling which held an unfinished blanket in the making and a sewing machine in this room and there was a room set aside for guests. This room contained two beds furnished with a mattress, feather bed, and two pillows each and there was always an excess of linen for visitors. The hallway was wide and the trunks and other odds and ends were kept there. It led to the front and back porches. The back porch was adjacent to the kitchen which had a pantry in which cooking utensils were kept; and the kitchen had a long table that would seat the entire family, a stove with a reservoir and warming closet for the food, a bench, and several chairs. In close proximity was a dinner bell which was rung at noon to alert the neighborhood that it was time to take a dinner and rest period until two o'clock when it would ring again for the return to work.

My family made do with the scarcity of living quarters because the landlord, Mr. Rackley, did not see fit to extend the living space. It was very difficult, especially during the hot summer months, and though my parents were his greatest asset and it was from them that he received his greatest amount of money during the harvest season, he never responded to pleas for more room.

Hazel Coley-Greene

Chapter Two

School Days

I remember walking to school on my first day with my brothers, which was about two and a half miles from home. I recall that there were farmhouses of both black and white all along the route. There was a white farmer and his sons who owned a cotton gin and he serviced the people in the neighborhood. He was a well-to-do landlord who had built homes for his sons and daughter in close proximity. There was also a block of landowners further down the road and I remember that a creek divided the two. They owned some hunting dogs, which would frighten the children by barking at them in the morning. I was especially afraid of them when they would chase my brothers and the children who were our neighbors.

The oldest brother, George Emmett, would carry the dinner pail and upon entering school, the pails were placed on a special bench until noon. The children would remove their topcoats and hang them on a nail in back of the room. Then they would take their seat. If the coats were wet, they would be placed by the stove to dry.

The school day would begin with a prayer led by the teacher, a bible selection such as the 23rd, 24th or 31st or 100th chapter of the Book of Psalms, which the children would repeat after her, followed by a song like Onward Christian Soldiers or the National Anthem. After this she would do a roll call and register the new students beginning with the smaller children.

When noon came and it was time to eat, our food would consist of what we had left over from breakfast such as ham, biscuits with butter, and a piece of cake or pie. All of the food was originally placed in one huge pail for the boys by my mother and the eldest brother would divide the food in parts for all of them. He did not divide it equally, but as he saw fit and when one brother complained to Mother that they were not getting their fair share of the food, she gave them separate pails. Since I was a girl, she bought me a beautiful lunch basket for me to carry my food in, but I was very tomboyish and would kick it on the way home like a football. It was delicate and was soon demolished beyond use and she was forced to give me a pail like the others.

  I started school at the age of six and my first thought as far as I can remember was that I was afraid of the teacher, wondering what she would look like and what her reactions to me would be. When I first saw her, she did not have a smile on her face. Then she finally smiled and that first impression was a lasting one and my fear was moderated considerably as time passed on. Then there were the students, most of which were strangers to me, but I gradually became accustomed to them. In the meantime, my eldest brother had difficulty trying to play with his friends. In the midst of the play period, he would look up and see me alone and weeping and that would spoil his fun for the remainder of the recess. He would come home and tell my mother and she would try to help me by talking to me, but that helped very little. This went on for a short while; then I began to make friends. We would play "House." The oldest girls would be the mother and the younger ones, the baby, and always I, would be the mother's helper. Other games we played were "Hide and Go Seek," "Dropping the Switch," and "Ring Around the Roses." The recess lasted for one and a half hours and after that, the bell would ring and the children would line up on either side of the steps—the boys on the right and the girls on the left and my line would always be the first to walk into the building.

  The small classroom with one teacher made it virtually impossible to make much progress and many classes were held only once or twice a week. I do not remember when and how I learned the alphabet or when I learned to read or write, but one of my brothers told me that the first word I learned to spell was SOAP from the box cover. My father used to have me reading for long periods of time in front of friends and relatives. I must have inherited my passion for reading from him. I remember how tired I used to get, but I would never complain. My audience was very receptive and I could not afford to disappoint them. There was a spelling bee given by the school in which I would always take part because I was very good with spelling words that I had read. The multiplication tables were routine for all students and we had to repeat and repeat them aloud until they were mastered and we learned to add, multiply, divide, and subtract as a result of a good knowledge of timetables. Our study of geography was frequent enough to allow us to learn some of the states and capitals as well as the rivers, lakes, and oceans.

We used chalk for writing on the board and pencils and paper instead of individual slate boards that my parents had used when they attended elementary school and it was more economical and easily handled by the students. The books were provided by the Board of Education and were used by all the students in the state of North Carolina. The name of our school was Exum Elementary Public School. It was the only school for blacks for many miles around. The enrollment was enormous and it was a small one-room office with three windows, one on each side and back, and a front door. It had a large wood-burning heater in the center which furnished ample heat for the one room. This little school was located on the farm of a Dr. Wyatt Exum for whom it was named. He was one of the physicians of the neighborhood who had a clientele for many miles, black and white alike, and our family was acquainted with him. It was situated in the center of about an acre of land and there were two outdoor toilets—one for the boys and one for the girls. They were grossly unsanitary but that was the best that we had. A ball diamond was made on the grounds by the students and a pump had been put in to furnish us with freshwater to drink and wash our hands. There was also a row of pine trees and sweet gum trees. Several of the pine trees emitted a resin and some of the students, especially boys, would pluck this resin and use it for chewing gum. In the woods there were vines on which small black balls grew and the boys discovered that these balls contained a seed that was covered with rubber substance. They would strip the outer layer from the balls and mix it with the resin or sweet gum and produce a bubble gum larger and more durable than that which we have on the market today.

As I remember, I went into the first grade at the time when there was no kindergarten because there was not enough time in the day for that. Actually there was not enough time for daily classes and following recess school would stay in until 3:00 PM, then the children would go home for the day. There were many times when the rain would be pouring down and it was necessary for us to go home in it. Some children were fortunate and would be driven home by horse and buggy, but for the most part they, too, would walk in the rain, but I do remember being driven home a few times. At the end of the week, there would be a Friday afternoon exercise of recitation, songs, spelling, and storytelling. This was an incentive for the power of self-expression and creativity and served as a helpful preparation for the Grand County Commencement which was held in the later years in the spring to test the progress and ability of the students who were to appear before the public. My early school years did not afford many good friends. I was not one for making friends easily and a great deal of it was due to my timidity. I favored reading and dramatics in my early school years and for games I liked Hide and Go Seek, but as I grew baseball became my game and I played with the boys and the girls. I held different bases and I was a good runner. I would catch the ball many times in the lap of my dress. The summer vacation did not offer much pleasure. I, with the rest of my family, was almost always overwhelmed with work on the farm tending and housing the crops and farm products.

I was always glad to see the vacation end, but my heart went out for those who were left behind and not able to attend school. During the summer, on Sundays, my parents would attend the Primitive Baptist Church where no children were affiliated. We were left to do the Sunday chores such as preparing dinner, tending to the cattle, watching the younger children, or tidying up the house. When that was finished, we would amuse ourselves by playing ball or playing house or playing with the neighbor's children or among ourselves. Many times we would roam the woods and fields searching for berries, gum, wildflowers, small animals, and birds, and I was such a tomboy that I tried to climb many trees looking for vines to make jumping ropes.

Hazel Coley-Greene

Elementary School class, 1926
(middle row 4th from right)

Occasionally our parents would take us to church with them after we had purchased our car. That was very enjoyable because we got dressed in our best clothes and went visiting our relatives and friends. The Missionary Baptist Churches were reserved for the black people who taught Sunday school to the children, but we did not have that privilege. Sometimes we would be allowed to attend Mount Pleasant Baptist Church on Children's Day where we took part in the program by reciting poems and verses that we had learned for the occasion, and sometimes on the second Sunday in May at that church, there was a quarterly meeting that we were allowed to attend.

The most disappointing time I remember from my early years was the fact that I remained in the fourth grade for four years. During that time, new teachers would be appointed to the school board each year and at no time was there an attempt to find out what my progress in those years had been. So at the end of the fourth year, I decided to go to the fifth grade. I was thirteen years old. My lack of promotion from year to year resulted in my being sixteen years old when I entered the eighth grade which was done without a certificate of promotion, just a declaration that I was in the eighth grade.

My family lived on the Rackley Plantation from 1898 until 1922. It was well after the birth of the last child who was then about seven years old. It was then that my father located his own tract of land, so we moved into the Buck Swamp Township in the vicinity of Pikeville, North Carolina. This move was not very productive for the family. My father had a stroke during that time and that was when my mother was forced to take the lead on the farm with her elder sons. There was not enough farming land to grow sufficient crops and my brothers spent much time clearing new ground and it was during this time that they were growing into manhood and were thinking of going out on their own. So it was not long before we found out that we could no longer live on our newly purchased farm and that was the beginning of the loss of most of our possessions. We started with 183 3/8 acres of land and lost all but forty-one acres.

In this neighborhood, I found the same type of one-room school which I had left behind with only one teacher. There were many new faces and many were strange. It was called Bunn Elementary School and at this time I was fourteen years old and in the sixth grade. The chances of educational advancement were about on the same par as the school I formerly attended. There was no birthday celebration as I can remember in my teen years. We were so busy that we did not realize that it happened, but I felt an added burden upon becoming a teenager because my mother would always remind me that I was a year older, which meant increased responsibilities. When I attended Bunn Elementary, I made friends with the McKennie family and the daughter, Pearl, became my best friend and we remain friends even now. My older brothers were no longer in school. Ronald, my youngest, was the only one and of course, the girls. This was a two teacher school and during this time, county commencements came into being.

Many schools met at a central location called Vail School. It was an elementary school of greater magnitude and of many teachers with outdoor exercises such as high jumping, relay racing, and ball games during the morning hours; and the afternoon session began immediately after lunch and lasted well into the day. The contests were of participants of many schools of many districts. There were contests in reading, spelling, storytelling, and in the explanation of anything that was executed with a special skill. There was a roster of judges for the participants of each contest and the winners would be awarded a prize. My brother, Ronald, won the first prize for explaining how to drive a Ford automobile. He also told of predictions that someday people would be driving automobiles of various colors on thorough ways throughout the United States. The audience was well amused and captivated and my mother smiled graciously when she was congratulated on the victory and imagination of her son. The closing number would be a presentation by the guest speaker who was invited for the occasion. He was Captain Hall, a fair demonstration agent for many counties, invited by Mrs. Maude Kenozie the County Supervisor, who was responsible for the success of this commencement.

Many parents and students met at this affair and some made lifelong acquaintances. This was an annual event that was greatly appreciated by many of the parents of the various school districts who attended in great numbers. The food served during these functions was phenomenal. It consisted of chicken, roasted pork, sausage, beef patties, potato and corn salad, cakes, pies, and pudding. The parents took great pride in the preparation of the food in their homes just for this occasion. When I reached the age of sixteen, my mother, being influenced by my Aunt Nancy, became interested in my entering high school. It was not a junior high school and it was located in Goldsboro on Elm Street in an area of town called Little Washington with a capacity of more than a thousand students. It was named for the first principal of the school, the Reverend Clarence Henry Dillard, and the present day principal was Professor Hugh Victor Brown. There was no integration at this time and the high school for the whites was in a different location in the city.

It was the year of 1924 when I was permitted to live with my Aunt Nancy so I could go to school. Upon entering the school at the age of sixteen, I was a bit apprehensive about giving my name as an eight grade student without a report card. Then, too, I was older and larger than the eight graders in my class. Mrs. Julia Hagens was the teacher in charge and when my name was called, I went up to her desk. She asked me for my report card as she had done with the other students and I said, "I do not have a report card but I am in the eighth grade." She looked at me for a moment, then without further questioning, she permitted me to pass to the eighth grade.

At the end of the week, I returned home in the rural area to see my parents. My mother asked me what grade did I make and I was proud to announce that I was in the eighth grade. She was surprised and shocked but very happy for me. I was either the first or second of her children to enter high school.

Entering high school opened up a vista and an appreciation of knowledge to which I had never been exposed. One advantage was that many subjects were as new to the other students in my class as they were to me such as algebra, literature, home economics, world history, etc. Consequently I was able to follow very well. If a student had a good average during the year, he or she would be exempt from the exams at the end of the term. I happened to be one of the exempt ones in several courses and that gave me a great deal of confidence in my ability to pursue my courses with less difficulty and greater self-assurance.

To transfer to a city school from a rural district was not as simple as one might have thought. On the weekend I would dread returning to a poorly lighted home with kerosene lamps and the dark interior walls and the low temperature of the room heated only by fireplaces. We lived so many blocks from anyone and outside, there was utter darkness, but I made the best of it. In the city, my Aunt Nancy had several neighbors and there was never any darkness because of the street lights. Even the local grocery stores and businesses were lighted up at night.

Entering the auditorium on my first day in school, I was very happy to see students and teachers performing their tasks with such ease. I recall that during that year, we presented a Japanese play under the direction of Miss Charity Hatcher. The auditorium was beautifully lighted, the stage decorated, and the participants were dressed and able to perform to perfection, I thought. I enjoyed the action from beginning to end and wondered if I would ever get a chance to be a part of such a production. It all seemed so strange to me and so out of my reach. On the way home I could think of nothing else. I was really impressed with the players. I daydreamed of being on the stage speaking and performing well-versed lines and being admired by the audience.

Reality set in at the close of the term when I returned to the farm to begin my chores. They consisted of chopping cotton, pulling totter, chopping and picking the worms off the tobacco leaves, and picking cotton as well as the house chores of laundry, preserving fruit, and plucking geese feathers for the beds. I also spent time with the rest of the family in the woods gathering blueberries for canning and for the market. We would sell them and use the money to buy material for dresses for church and special occasions. My sister, Pocahontas, was able to cut and fit and sew beautifully. Mine were poorly made and she always had to help me finish. Our shoe supply consisted of a pair for winter and a pair for summer and Sundays. During the week we usually went in our bare feet and many times our summer shoes would become too tight. Another source of money came from the sale of milk and butter. My brother, Edmond, was designated for this job. My mother always had milking cows so we always had a surplus for sale.

The following fall, the second year of my high school term, I was a full pledged second year student, a sophomore, and happy to reunite with all of my classmates. The preparations for returning to the city from the rural area were far less difficult than the previous year. I kinda felt like one of the gang. I was able to follow in class with ease and my only hang-up was having to go home for the weekend. However, I tried to manifest a good spirit which brought happiness to my family. During the summer of that year, I worked on the farm as usual, but I remember being bitten on my hip by a spider. I had to be taken to see Dr. Bryant in the city and he gave me an injection for the pain which lasted about two days. That very same weekend, my grandmother Coley died, so the family was involved with her burial as well as my mishap.

School opened in September and I was now a junior and I felt well on my way and stood shoulder to shoulder with the other students of my class. I had captured the love and respect of the principal, Professor H.V. Brown; Alice Brown, his wife; my English teacher,

Miss Charity Hatcher; my history teacher, Miss Rosa Gray; and many other of the teachers in school. These scholars were a great inspiration to me and aided me in developing a deep appreciation for Negro womanhood. But, most of all, Alice Brown assumed a motherly attitude toward me, which gave me an untold strength and confidence, which went a long way in the development of the stamina which carried me over deep waters during my lifetime.

One day during the latter part of September in 1926, a note was delivered to my English teacher, Mrs. Wilks, which was a shock to all of the rural students attending Dillard High School. It read: All rural students attending Dillard High School will be suspended as of today because of the lack of space to accommodate them. It was signed by the Superintendent of Schools, Mr. Armstrong. She read the note with no sign of remorse and quickly gave it back to the bearer and resumed her classroom duties. I hardly think she realized what a blow it dealt to many of the students at the sound of her voice. To me it was like a bombshell that had exploded and shattered my plans for an education. My first impulse was to resort to tears. I did not strongly dislike this teacher but there was no great love for her either.

That same day my mother was in the city with the family attending the funeral of our cousin. I also attended and was overwhelmed with tears so much so that my mother sensed that something was wrong which was not related to the death. She quickly questioned me as to what was troubling me and I told her that I could no longer attend school in the city. I told her that the system is suspending all rural children because of lack of space. My mother immediately said, "Don't cry, dear, you will go to school."

In the meantime, Mr. H. V. Brown had heard of our plight and wrote a letter to the wife of Captain Hall—the state farm demonstrator who lived in Raleigh—to see if she might need some domestic help in her home which would allow me to attend Washington High School in that city. She stated in the letter that I was a jewel and I would be a great help to her. Mrs. Hall granted me an interview but she was not interested in any domestic help at that time. My two brothers and Uncle Needham were in Raleigh at that time and resided in the Lewis Hotel which had been constructed by him when he was in the bricklaying business. They were able to contact a training school called Berry O'Kelley Training School in Method, North Carolina, and enrolled me in the junior class there.

This was an entirely new experience. I was placed in a frame building in a room with five other young ladies. These ladies became almost like sisters to me. There were three beds with two ladies per bed. My bedmate was Clydie Dunn, but my closest friend was Alfreda Hill. The others were Maxie Dalton, Elizabeth Morgan, and Marjorie Hunt. My friend Alfreda taught me how to play the ukulele so I bought one and took it home that Christmas. One day, Alfreda said to me, "I don't like the name Ethelene. I think I'm going to call you Hazel" and Hazel it became from then to this day. I just moved Ethelene into the middle of my name and that was that. When the junior class met, I was there and felt very much at home. I had started school that year about three weeks ahead of this group of students. Consequently I was a jump ahead of them and appeared to be a little more advanced, which was an advantage, but not really true.

As the classes met from day to day, I soon became acquainted with all of my instructors and they were all very cordial to me and some were particularly easy to reach. Mr. Smith was my algebra instructor and he headed the debating team. I joined along with Elisa Weaver and we were part of the team that defeated the opposing team from the Agricultural and Technical College in Greensboro, North Carolina, that year. The school officials were overjoyed with the success. Mr. Cox, our principal, and Mr. Berry O'Kelley, the founder of our school, extended an honorable mention to us at an assembly in the auditorium.

I was very popular at Berry O'Kelley School and my self-esteem increased considerably. I was happier than I had ever been in school. The scholastic atmosphere far surpassed that which existed in the Goldsboro High School. In other words, I felt like one of the group. During the Easter vacation, one of my roommates invited me to spend the holiday in her home in Zebulon, North Carolina. With the permission of my mother, the school granted the request, so my brothers Emmett and Freeman took me downtown in Raleigh to purchase a coat, dress, and some shoes for the trip. I graciously enjoyed the holiday and the generous hospitality of all whom I met.

When I returned to school, the preparations were being considered for the end-of-the-year school play and I was chosen as a participant. It was beautifully done and apparently enjoyed by all who attended. The final examinations preceded the school closing exercises and I was relieved of the stress and anxiety that exams cause any student. A young man and I became friends before the closing of school. His name was McCoy. We corresponded during the summer months with the idea of reuniting in the fall, but that did not come to pass. I had, in fact, said good-bye to all of my friends.

At the end of that school year, I had been promoted to the senior class and I felt that I was well on my way. I went home and resumed the chores of the farm which were becoming more burdensome and unpleasant than ever before. I was becoming more and more alienated from those drudged farm tasks as the years passed. My father and mother had grown weaker and the farm help was not as abundant as before. My sister Pocahontas was kept out of high school the year I was away at Berry O'Kelley because of the extreme poor health of my mother.

The following school year, I returned to Dillard High School as a senior and my sister enrolled at Berry O'Kelley Training School. I did not regain the enthusiasm I had when I was in Berry O'Kelley, but I was happy to be in school and I made use of the opportunity. I was a member of the debating team and the Dramatics Club and was very active in both. That same year, Mother was treated by a Dr. Plommerent and the treatment proved to be very helpful to her. As I was finishing my last year at Dillard, I was still going home on the weekends to the rural area to try and make it more livable for the family. My younger brother Ronald and sister Clara were still in elementary school and in the spring, my mother returned home which made life much more pleasant. On May 28, 1929, I graduated from Dillard High School at the age of twenty. During that year, I met Albert Drawhorn, who was helping me adjust to city life and we remained friends even when I went to college. My Uncle Needham became interested in my seeking higher education and was the one who interceded in my enrollment at Shaw University in Raleigh, North Carolina—a college of about 350 students. The cost to attend was about $30.00 per month.

My plans before my uncle intervened were that of a different nature. I had considered enrolling in a school of nursing and becoming a registered nurse. My uncle had heard of some weird tales of nurses and doctors and he felt that to obtain a college education would be a far greater value than becoming a registered nurse. I accepted his advice and decided to pursue a college degree.

For the first time, he invited me to live with him and his family and I would be responsible for some of the chores around the home. At that time, I was without sufficient clothes for school so he supplied me with a raincoat and some overshoes. He did not realize that a freshman in college had many needs for many things but we did the best we could with the money afforded. He and I would do the marketing for the week on Saturday mornings and I would clean the living quarters and I was also expected to attend church on Sunday.

About midway of the school year, his building construction and brick mason business called him to Washington, D.C. and it would be necessary for him to be there for several months. Upon his return, some neighbors reported that I was roaming the streets instead of studying which was untrue but how was he to know. I had returned to the farm to help for the summer and during my absence, he decided that I should reside in the dormitory, Estey Hall, which he called "Ester." I welcomed the move and resided on the Shaw University campus from 1929 to 1932 when I graduated. My tuition and board were paid by him regularly each month for the years that I was there.

Hazel age 20, Senior at Dillard High School

Dillard High School
Goldsboro, North Carolina

DIPLOMA

This Diploma Certifies, that Hazelle Ethelene Coley has completed the Course of Study prescribed for the High School of this City by the Board of Trustees, and is entitled to all the honors and privileges of a Graduate of this Institution.

High School Diploma, May 28, 1928

I was able to secure small chores around the school for spending money such as waiting tables and as house girl to the Dean of Women, Mrs. Lillie V. Rivers. My major in college was Chemistry with a minor in Biological Sciences. I chose these courses because they were more interesting to me and the experiments eliminated a great deal of reading and writing which I did not care to do. My favorite professors were Dr. J. Thomas Fortone Fletcher, Dr. Nelson Harris, and Dr. Wonthaw. These three professors showed an interest in me that I did not find in my other instructors, but frankly, I do not feel that any one instructor directly influenced my decisions of life.

During that year as I joined the campus group, I met and began to associate with the young ladies and gentlemen of the campus. I was better able to attend functions given by the school such as concerts, plays, basketball, and football games. My roommate was Miss Naomi Lennon. She had a brother in The Lester School on the football team and he and I became close, long-lasting friends. My friendship with the males did not develop rapidly that year, but I became friends with many.

With all the happiness that these experiences afforded, there was always a note of sadness that accompanied it and that was that my older brothers were robbed of such an opportunity to participate in college life and the extracurricular activities that go along with it. During this time, my two sisters, Pocahontas and Clara, and my brother Ronald were well on their way in high school. In fact, my sister Poke was graduating that year.

At the close of my second year, as usual, I returned home to work on the farm. I found my sister had indeed graduated and was making preparations to go to Washington, D.C. to seek employment. She persuaded me to go with her, so we set out together with no work experience. We spent several nights at the YMCA and then went out on jobs as domestic workers—she at $8.50 per week and I at $10.00. She was working in D.C. and I was located with Mrs. William E. Lee in Bethesda, Maryland, that summer and I did many chores such as cooking and helping with her five children. When I was ready to return to school, my uncle wanted my sister Poke to attend Shaw with me, but she had other plans which included another school, Howard University, so she matriculated there and I returned to Raleigh alone.

This would be my third year at school and it was a beautiful year. My acquaintance with a male student was increasing. Vincent Samuel Greene from Brooklyn, New York, was my secret passion. He was a very brilliant student and was a student leader. He was well-versed and played the violin beautifully. He was a member of the Phi Beta Sigma Fraternity, a Sigma man.

During the year, I studied history for six weeks at the Agricultural and Technical College in Greensboro as an exchange student and during my stay there, I contacted Mrs. Lee who hired me to stay with her children while she and her husband went to the Boise, Idaho, homestead. This entailed a great responsibility; however, I was able to manage successfully and was hoping she would give me a bonus of some sort for assuming the responsibility for her home and children, but she did not. She was only interested in the welfare of her family.

When I left my sister, Poke went to work with her, but they did not get along very well. Her rules were more on the slave and master type which we were not accustomed to. She realized her disposition when my sister told her what an inconsiderate and hard-hearted person she was. She was reluctant in giving her enough to eat or time to rest, but before the conference was over between them, she admitted that she was crueler than she realized and prevailed upon my sister to give her another chance, but my sister went back to D.C. anyway.

Chapter Three
Leaving Childhood

I went back to school as a senior. Vincent and I began to spend more and more time together. I pledged the Zeta Phi Beta Sorority and became a sister to the Phi Beta Sigma Fraternity. Very often he would serenade me with his violin music at night and he allowed me to wear his fraternity pin. I felt very secure with him. In the meantime, he had not severed his former female connections and I was still in contact with my other male friends, especially Garland. Vincent spent two and a half years in college at Shaw but was unable to complete the courses there because of lack of funds.

During the spring of my last year in school, Professor Harris held an extension course in Goldsboro, North Carolina, and at that time my family lived in walking distance of the school and with the permission of the Dean of Women, I was able to attend classes and visit quite often.

It is a tradition that during the closing exercises, all upperclassmen would participate in the program. I enjoyed the participation in my junior year, but it was my turn now and the enjoyment was even sharper. The play that year was Antigone, directed by Dr. T. Thomas Fortune Fletcher in which, of course, I participated.

Then, graduation day came, May 28, 1932, and the hustle and bustle of getting ready for the march was very exciting. Dawning a cap and gown on Graduation Day is an event which every graduate looks forward to and the enjoyment of the very act of doing so; then that final march of each student, one by one to the roster to receive a diploma which represented four years of "faithful work worthy of success" as our class motto stated and repeated so eloquently by our valedictorian, Mr. Garland Crews, in his farewell address. Then there is a realization of a sudden change of lifestyle which unlocks the arms of protection about one and throws one into the fields of harvesting alone.

Since I had not obtained employment in the educational field after a few days of preparation to vacate the college, I decided to go to New York City and seek employment there. Having no experience, I was forced to take a job as a domestic/governess working at $35.00 per month. The economy was at a very low ebb then. My charge was a lovely little girl who called me Hazel. Her parents never seemed to have enough time for her and she was always lonely. We would take long walks on Fifth Avenue and look into the store windows.

I remember telling her that someday I would marry a doctor and have a little girl of my own and that we would travel and purchase wonderful fabric in open air markets. One evening as she and her parents were having dinner she repeated what I had said and the mother blurted out, "So Hazel is going to marry a doctor!"

After a few weeks, I was able to find my way around fairly well and Vincent and I spent enough time together to become very well acquainted. Everyone was very cordial and, in fact, Mrs. Samuel Greene introduced me to friends and family as her future daughter-in-law. I was a guest at the church picnic and in the evenings, we would go dancing at Big Wilt's Small's Paradise or take in a show at the Apollo on 125th Street.

At the end of the summer, I returned to my home state and with the recommendation of Professor Nelson Harris, the educational director in Raleigh, I secured a teaching position. It was an all new experience for me. I was placed as a third grade teacher in the Freemont School System under the direction of Professor E. A. Cheek. With thirty-five children under my control in the auditorium with several exits, some leading to the outside and some leading to adjacent classrooms, it was a problem in the beginning. The children were distracted by the interference of someone entering at frequent intervals, but this was corrected within a few weeks and we were able to get down to business in spite the disturbances.

SENIOR CLASS, 1932

Shaw University, Graduation Day—May 28, 1932

College Degree, June 1, 1932

Since I had obtained a degree for teaching high school biology, it was a disappointment to be categorized as an elementary school teacher making $30.00 a month, but it was necessary to make the best of the situation and the school term was successful. The discipline was satisfactory and the children were eager to pass from the third to the fourth grade without much problem.

During that year, Vincent visited my home and met my parents. While he was talking to them, I was in the kitchen struggling to fry enough chicken for dinner. I wasn't very adroit in the preparation of a meal so at the table, my mother apologized for the crispy fowl. Vincent smiled, bit into a drumstick, and said, "Best I ever ate." They liked him and he liked them. While he was visiting during that summer, he asked my mother if he might marry me and it was agreed. I was sorry that he did not include both of my parents, but it was customary that the mother be asked on such matters. My father later mentioned a feeling of being left out and unfortunately he died before I had the opportunity to make it up to him and I always regretted it.

Each teacher was responsible for a closing exercise at the end of the term. For my class, I chose the marriage of Jack and Jill. Every child in the class was incorporated into the program from the bride and groom to the ushers. It was beautiful to see all the children in action. It added self-esteem to each of them and the parents were overjoyed and expressed a deep appreciation for the motivation of their children. The faculty was also very supportive, which made the evening run very smoothly; and all who attended apparently had an enjoyable time. My mother attended. She was surprised to learn that I had made all of the costumes, which was quite an order considering none of the parents were able to help me. When it was all over, I was unable to sleep wondering all night how I had been able to pull it off.

After spending a few days with my family in Goldsboro, I returned to New York City. Vincent and I spent a great deal of time together making plans for the upcoming marriage. We had lots of fun although in the midst of the recession and there was no money to have. We would walk down Seventh Avenue to 125th Street, go into Bloomsteen's Department Store, and choose all of the items we wanted in our first home. Of course, we didn't purchase a thing, but it was such an enjoyable time. I had been re-hired by the same school district again, but in the rural area in a two-room house, which would be quite a contrast to the previous school year.

Walking down Seventh Avenue circa, 1935

My time in New York was running out, so we married on September 16, 1936, in the home of the Reverend Eldridge, pastor of the church the Greene family attended. We were accompanied by the matron of honor, Miss Rebecca Langford, and the best man, Charlie Greene, his brother. Though it was small, it was exciting. I wore a long blue satin gown that I had fashioned myself and it was tailored wonderfully to fit my shape. The news had reached Mrs. Greene before we arrived at the house and they scolded us for not telling them. They had hoped for a church wedding but they recovered from their disappointment and wished us much love and happiness. We spent a very short honeymoon on Long Island and I was on my way back to North Carolina for my teaching assignment.

When I arrived home, I showed both my parents the wedding ring. They were surprised but happy. They, too, gave me their blessing and soon the entire family knew about it. News had reached the school before I did; however, it did not make a difference at all. I spent a fairly good year but it was not as spectacular as the previous one. I taught fourth through the seventh grade and, again, was paid $30.00 per month. The students were very cooperative and I was able to cover a reasonable amount of material which enabled me to promote all of them to an upper grade. My coworker, Mrs. Ida Belle Aldridge, and I lived near the school with a Mr. and Mrs. Green during the week and we would go home on weekends. During the Christmas holiday, Vincent came to North Carolina to spend time with me and my family. The time together was well spent and we visited family and relatives and enjoyed the Yuletide goodies with everyone. The New Year ushered in all too soon and he returned to his home and I started the second half of my school year, which ended almost without notice. The closing exercises were cut short because of rain, so a portion of it was held in a classroom. Very few parents attended and not all of the students. The fact that my teaching experience was not in the field for which I was prepared contributed to my not being able to develop an appreciation for the teaching profession, so I did not pursue it any further.

When I returned to New York, I spent one year sort of recuperating from the hustle and bustle of the previous years without a letup and to become acquainted with New York City. My husband and

I resided with his grandmother at the time. I had only been in the city about two weeks when my brother Leeman became ill and passed away and it became necessary for me to return home for the funeral. My father was ailing during that time, having been a victim of two episodes of CVA. He passed in July 1935, which necessitated another trip home.

In 1936 and 1937, I pursued a course in graduate school at Columbia University at Teacher's College majoring in Microbiology and Genetics. I attended for two semesters and received thrity-six hours towards a master's degree. My thoughts about the value of college in a person's life are that the value is immeasurable. There is always room at the top with many great opportunities waiting for one to attain. It increases self-esteem and strengthens the ability for leadership. I knew I would advise my children and grandchildren to obtain a college education if at all possible.

My expenses were paid because I was on a work program called the Work Progress Administration or W.P.A., sponsored by the government for the assistance to professional persons who had not had an opportunity to work in a professional capacity and in 1937 and 1938, we both established eligibility for full professional employment by the W.P.A. program. That same year, we moved from Grandmother's to our own apartment in the Harlem River Houses at 48 McCombs Place. I was on field activity and Vincent was in a recreational program in the schools.

Our closest friends were Olga and William Edwards and their three children, Delores and twins Joyce and Billy. We teased them because the baby boy was so much larger than his sister and crowded her in the carriage so much so that one could hardly see the little girl. They were a loving couple and nice to be around with and I longed for a family of my own.

Olga and William introduced us to Mr. A. Merrill Willis and sisters Edith and Ruth Baker who attempted to establish a Colonel Young Memorial Foundation affiliated with the Baptist ministries, but a conflict in ideas arose and we were forced to sever our connections. It was during this time that Vincent became interested in organizing the tenants of the Harlem River Houses into a tenants' association. He was very influential and the tenants rallied around him; however, it was a city housing project and a tenants' organization would not be tolerated so it was obligatory for us to seek other living quarters. We moved to the Paul Lawrence Dunbar Apartments and the tenants' association petered out. Soon afterwards, Vincent became affiliated with the textile workers union, AFL-CIO which afforded him a lucrative employment. I became employed by the War Department in Harbor Side, New Jersey, which was a task force center in 1942.

Mrs. Vincent Samuel Greene—Elementary School Teacher, 1937

From the beginning, when I became acquainted with Vincent, he and I had discussed his desire to become a physician and in college, I remember him saying that his mother wanted him to be a doctor and he did not want to disappoint her; but as the time passed, he became less and less enthusiastic. He was a mediator for the AFL-CIO and was quite secure in his position. I wanted to be a doctor's wife so I tried to encourage him to reconsider and seriously think about returning to college, but we started having small arguments about it and we were getting nowhere. He finally said that it was not the right time for him to study medicine since he had finally landed a good paying position and we were financially secure. So I placed my hands on my hips and said, "If you won't, I will." He said, "Baby, do you want to study medicine?" I said, "Yes." He looked at me with dismay and said, "More power to you." So it all started, just like that. From that very night, we began to think of all that would have to be done before I could get started. First of all, my college transcript had to be evaluated. There were no credits for physics. I had dropped the class, so while still employed with the War Department, I attended City College of New York and studied physics at night.

At the time my mother was visiting with us and to work during the day, attend school in the evening, and come home to her after having been away the entire day was a difficult chore, but she needed some companionship and I gave her some each night as well as comb her long tresses. At this point, I did not know where I would be studying medicine. I decided that if I took some refresher courses at Howard University in Washington, D.C., I would perhaps be able to make my way into the Howard Medical School.

While there, I was residing with Dean Dowling, the Dean of the School of Engineering. I felt that since I was part of his household, he would have spoken to the board on my behalf, but he flatly refused and said that I had personality and that I was forward enough to act on my own. There were also other obstacles. It was 1940 and schools were infiltrated with former soldiers who had preference over the civilian population.

Chapter Four

The Tide Turns

I was able to pursue another course in physics and to review some chemistry, but that was as far as I was able to go. I took the Medical Aptitude Test but that did not enhance my progress.

My cousin, Lydia Singleton, was a young college student at the time, a brilliant and very determined young lady. She completed her college courses, studied law, and became an attorney. Both of us had admiration for each other. She often said that at the time that I returned to school, it was not popular for a person to have been out of school for eighteen years and return for the purpose of pursuing a course of study in medicine.

She became acquainted with Clarence Wilson, who was a pre-med student at the time and went on to become a doctor of medicine. They married and she became a counselor at law. I lost track of them when I returned to New York, but Dr. Wilson visited me on occasions and informed me of George Cunningham who was pursuing a course in medicine at the Free University of Brussels in Belgium. He made it possible for me to contact him and I did so immediately. Cunningham gladly assisted me in establishing contact and enrolling in the medical school.

During the process of our preparation for entrance into a European medical school, an urgent coincidence happened in our lives. A little girl was born in the family, a niece, that her father, my brother Emmett named Lillie after our mother, and placed her in the care of my sister Clara in Goldsboro, North Carolina. At this time, Clara was married and a very successful hairdresser and had the means to care for the infant. However, the child's mother saw her one day and how well she was thriving and demanded her return. Having no legal recourse, the little girl went back to her birth mother, a fifteen-year-old, who was ill-prepared to care for an additional child. Her mother, a young woman from Crenshaw, South Carolina, named Maggie Bowden had recently died and left her children to be cared for by her working husband and the young girl. While she was away at school, the other children would eat the baby's food and drink the milk and soon the child became malnourished and ill. So the infant was taken by her father and returned to his sister's home. Fearing that the same thing would happen again once the baby was healthy, my brother and sister decided to call me in New York and set up a plan of action.

Vincent and I traveled to Goldsboro with good intentions and the moment I set eyes on that little girl, I knew she would be the joy of my life and that I would never be alone in life. I nicknamed her "Butchie" because we had not yet decided on a first name. I wanted it to be Bettye Ann but several discrepancies arose which thawed our attempts to go through with the adoption; however, we were able to obtain a change of name from Lillie Elizabeth Bowden to that of Lillie Coley-Greene. My husband did not like the name Bettye. The Coley family name was her heritage and the most important part of the name, but the Greene was important also because Vincent had gladly consented to it all. This was reconfirmed in 1974 by Attorney Richard E. Nettum, a necessary act, because all traces of the name change were lost and were never found. So from the very beginning, she was a blood relative, but at the age of two, she became family, the daughter of Hazel and Vincent Greene and we were proud.

In 1950, my mother who had been living with my sister Clara came to live with us. It became quite a challenge to care for a septuagenarian and a busy child. We were living in a two-bedroom, one-bath apartment, so some changes had to be made. We transformed our dining room into a master bedroom and gave both Mother and Butchie a room respectively. Sometimes during the night, our little girl would crawl into bed with her grandmother and I would find them both wet in the morning. There was lots of love between those two and I saw a side of my mother I had never seen before. In the morning, she would comb her thinning hair and dress it in two long braids that she would pin across the top of her head.

Many times Butchie would take the brush and attempt to help and tangle it in her hair. Mother did not seem disturbed by her actions although I am sure it was painful.

Vincent purchased a RCA television and we would sit together in the living room and watch the limited programming. Mother's vision was beginning to fade so I would read to her and reminisce about the family, the farm, and our neighbors. Oftentimes we would sing some church hymns together and I would try to imitate Ella Fitzgerald's "A Tisket a Tasket" that we would hear on the radio. Our relationship had changed over the years and although the love was always there, now we had a newfound respect for each other. Vincent called her "Mother Coley" and would always make her laugh. I do not remember her laughing much when I was a child except maybe with the boys. On Saturday afternoon, my husband would take us for a ride through Central Park and down Fifth Avenue and although she could not see much, she enjoyed being out and riding with the windows open.

Some Sunday mornings, Vincent would go to a fishing spot on the Hudson, catch some eel, and we would have fried eel, scrambled eggs, grits, and biscuits for breakfast. I always asked him to skin them before bringing them home because I just could not do it. Also, during those days, we were watching the presidential campaign very closely. Vincent and Mother were saying, "I like Ike." I, on the other hand, was an Adlai Stevenson girl, Democrat all the way; but I never got a chance to vote that year because of a change in plans and it was with much regret that I had to see her leave when Ronald drove up from North Carolina to take her back home with him. I had been accepted in the Université Libre de Bruxelles for matriculation in 1951, but it was actually September 12, 1952, when I set sail because of some financial difficulties, the anxiety, and the actual decision to go. Having never been on a long distance voyage, it was a little difficult to make up my mind to make a transatlantic trip of three thousand miles and yet it was necessary if I was to reach my destination. Since I did not present myself as a student in 1951, I requested another chance in 1952 and was immediately accepted.

Now I had no reason for further delay, so Vincent and I had no more time for preparation. The trip was on and I gave my daughter a going-away party decorated in yellow and blue and made her the cutest long yellow taffeta dress with a blue sash. Many times we passed the New York harbor en route to Brooklyn to visit my husband's family and our little girl would say, "Look, Mama, the Queen Mary is in" and knowing that we were to book passage on that ship would give me a feeling of anxiety. She had been told that we were sailing to Europe and that was something she was looking forward to with great anticipation. It required courage to make the preparations. I had graduated from college in 1932 and now it was 1952. Twenty years had gone by and now, I was about to depart from the known to travel to the unknown, away from family and friends to study medicine in a foreign country. Planning what items to take was a great task because not knowing what was available to us there made it that much more difficult and George Cunningham was not much help. He was a man. What did he know about a woman's necessities? I thought about toiletries, hair pomades, and straightening combs and what would I do when Butchie reached puberty? I already started sewing some items of clothing I knew for sure we would need for the trip over and I had bought enough underwear for a Girl Scout troop. I spent several weeks packing and going shopping under the bridge for our fashionable going-away outfits.

I designed a cute black—and white-checked coat for "Butchie" with a short cape collar and I would wear a chic gray suit with a peplum jacket split on the back seam and, of course, I had platform sling-back heels. She had her favorite patent leather strap shoes to complement the ensembles. My sister Clara arrived from Goldsboro with a case of sterno, Royal Crown hair grease, pressing combs, and curling irons and she also decided to include a converter in case Brussels was on DC current and we wanted to use the electric kind. She stayed up the night before pressing my hair and giving my daughter a million baby doll curls.

On the morning of departure, many friends from New York and Carolina gathered to see us off and took pictures in front of the Dunbar Apartments Leasing Office. My friends Gertrude Lowe and Leslie Ashby were there as well as my cousin Elise and many others. I don't remember why Vincent did not drive to the pier, but we all went by taxi and it was just as well because he gave us a champagne farewell party in our cabin and had a lot to drink.

Hazel and Lillie—Leaving for Europe—Sept 10, 1952

Finally the boat set sail and we watched and watched until we could no longer see our family and friends waving and it was strange to feel sorrow and excitement at the same time. I prayed for strength, faith, and understanding. This prayer was answered by a thought—"Thy faith is sufficient for thee that come to me"—words that I had not heard since I was a child from family members during prayer service in our home. Then too, my husband was an ardent supporter of the idea and helped me on every leg of the journey except he forgot to make the hotel reservation for a one-night stay in Paris before heading to Brussels the following day.

Onboard the ship, there were enough activities to keep us well entertained during our three-days-and-three-nights trip. Each day the table settings were with fresh flowers and an array of fruits like I had never seen. There were always activities for the children during the day and dancing and games at night for the adults. It was a beautiful experience, one which I will never forget.

When we were ready to dock, I could not find my child. When I did, she and some friends had gone to a movie at the last minute.

I was so angry. We got dressed and rushed to disembark with the other passengers. We boarded the boat train for a short trip to Paris where we had hotel reservations for the night. The following morning we got up early and ordered something to eat. I did not speak much French so I did the best I could. The concierge said he spoke Engleesh, so when I ordered some oatmeal, he heard "haut meek" and sent up hot milk. We were wondering why the milk in the glasses was not cold. After breakfast, we boarded the train from Paris to Brussels, Belgium and it was a relief to know that this was the last leg of our journey.

The trip through the countryside was very similar to that of the United States. I remember the apple trees laden with rich golden fruit, the animals grazing on the meadows, and the chickens in the farmyard were plentiful. About midway of our ride, dinner was served in the passenger car where we were seated. The abundance of red wine with the meal was very fascinating. Our train moved along swiftly and my greatest concern now was to reach our destination and meet George Cunningham.

Finally our train arrived at the terminal. It was on my anniversary, September 16, and Cunningham was there. We were happy to see each other. After exchanging greetings, we boarded a taxi and we were on our way. We drove by the Free University of Brussels and he informed me that there was the place that I would be going to class. A few butterflies fluttered in my stomach, but the feeling subsided.

We soon arrived in Ixelles, a suburb of Brussels. Our address was 40 Avenue Guillaume Macau where we met our proprietors, Madame and Monsieur Jacques Charletaux, and their little dog, Poum Poum, who became a constant companion to Lillie while she was waiting to be enrolled in school. The house had beautiful wooden floors covered with rich-looking area rugs that reminded me of tapestry. After all, we were on the old continent and valuable items were everyday ware. On the walls hung family portraits and many sconces with crystal globes. I often wondered what value one would put on such a house. Our room was on the 2nd floor and was just a "room". The toilet was in the hall. The only full bathroom was located on the 1st floor in the quarters of Monsieur le Docteur, and elderly gentleman who kept a room there for his infrequent visits to the city. His suite was on the first floor right beneath ours and we were told to use the tub during his absence; but I knew right away that I would have to purchase a huge tub so Lillie and I could bathe nightly in privacy.

Our meals would be eaten downstairs in the dining room and would be prepared by the lady of the house and her mother; but if we desired to do so, we could go down to the lower level where the kitchen and rear gardens were. The Charleteaux were very congenial people and told us to feel at home there and that they would do all they could to help us adjust. They were curious about every aspect of our lives and customs in the United States. They wanted to know how we got our hair straight and why our skin was not dark like the few Africans they had seen and what type of work my husband did, especially since I told them that he was not in the entertainment business and although they were being paid handsomely for their services, they taught and cared dearly for my child while I was engrossed in my studies.

Madeleine secured the services of a friend, a teacher, as a language tutor for us, and it was not long before I was able to enroll my child in school. Besides being lonely, occasionally she seemed to have a lot of fun playing with the little dog and walking in the gardens that were surrounded by an iron fence.

Lillie with Madame Madeleine Charleteaux

In the gardens at 40 Avenue Guillaume Macau, 1952

In the dining room, there was a huge table that had been carved quite intricately out of a single block of wood. It had been in Madeleine's mother's family since she was a young girl. The furniture in the sitting room was mahogany with burgundy velvet cushions and faced enormous glass patio doors that opened onto a small terrace overlooking the front gardens.

Our street was an avenue with rows of trees, not a long street but wide with plenty of room for ball playing, bicycle riding, and skating all of which Butchie would do quite frequently. The elementary school was located a block away and a little further were the lakes of Ixelles, a calm place with ducks, swans, and walkways. During our years in Brussels, we would often go there for some diversion or simply to find some peaceful moments. Adjacent to the lakes was the main thoroughfare, the Chausee d'Ixelles, where one could ride the tram, Brussels' public transportation to all points of the city. Many times my little girl and I would ride to the end of the line and back, talking and viewing all of the sights along the way. It was quite a ride and very enjoyable at a low cost. Brussels has a lot of memorable landmarks and beautifully illuminated at night. Years later my "Butchie" would study the history of Belgium and how all of these places were named and it was all so very fascinating. She once told me a story about the Roi Albert (King Albert). I thought she was saying wild bear. I just could not figure out where the beast fit in the dynasty of the Belgian royals, but she collected histories and photographs and recounted the actions with such enthusiasm and I was corrected.

From time to time, we would receive a package from Vincent with several delectable morsels and items we wanted to bring with us and could not find in Europe but were not essential at our time of departure. In one of the boxes, Vincent had included an old porcelain-faced Indian doll that his daughter cherished dearly, but during the shipping the face had broken into several pieces. She held the little broken doll in her arms and cried and cried and it was several days before her interest went elsewhere and the doll was forgotten. Fortunately, it was during this time that she made the acquaintance with Marguerite Vrooman, a little girl from The Netherlands, and she began to learn some Dutch language and mores of the people of the low country. Mrs. Vrooman, her mother, even taught her to knit with four needles and how to cross-stitch. I often wondered how they communicated since they both spoke little French.

At first it was all so strange. George spent much time acquainting me with some of the many things that would be confronting me. I remember the first medical book that I was introduced to was "Anatomy of The Upper and Lower Extremities." It was in French. I spent a great deal of time on the first few pages. Every word had to be translated so I could understand it. Imagine the colossal task I had facing me in the beginning.

Registration for classes was my next important step. Some classes were held in different buildings, which were located in different sections of the city, but many were held in the university building next to St. Pierre Hospital. The first class that I attended was Human Anatomy. It began as I remember on the first day of October in 1952. The instructor was Dr. Dalque, professor of anatomy. I remember I took a seat on the front row with the hope of a better understanding of what as going on. For several meetings, I did not understand what was being said, but one day I heard the word "phrenique" spoken in the lecture, so I went home and read all I could find regarding the phrenic nerve, which gave me some insight on that particular subject. There were many times that I was able to get a better understanding of the lecture in anatomy as well as the other subjects in the curriculum by using the above method. Many of the courses of study were made by assembling the notes of the lectures of the previous year into a course of study for the incoming students. They had been translated into English and were easy to read. One could purchase the course and obtain basic information in a particular course.

All foreign students who attempted the study of medicine at the Free University of Belgium were required to have graduated from a four-year college. This would enable them to be exempt from the first candidature of the medical course, leaving six more years of study to be done. These were divided into two years of study as a candidate and four doctoral years in a hospital, which were called the clinical years.

During the first year, there was more to be done than I had the time for, plus the fact that my daughter needed some of my time for partial orientation to an all-new situation in a foreign country, as well as the language barrier. The first few months, she cried to return home to her friends and classmates. Europeans did not celebrate Thanksgiving and she was especially sad during the first Christmas holiday season because the Belgian Santa was called St. Nicholas and visited the children on December 6, and not on December 25.

My class work had begun in October and ended in May. The last month was reserved for the students to do a thorough review of the years' work. It was called "Le mois de bloc," "cram month" in English. Actually, that June, I was not prepared for the examinations and did not pass. It was quite humiliating. Our first summer was a bit different. There was no Independence Day celebration, but we did learn about a national holiday on July 21. In New York we would go to the beach and Coney Island at least twice during the summer, but all of that was substituted by a school day camp and weeks of study. The daily temperature was around seventy degrees, so sometimes I would walk to the square and marvel at the array of vegetables and meats that were unavailable in my country.

The residents of Brussels were very clean people. Many times, one could see members of a household out front sweeping then actually scrubbing the sidewalks with soap and water. They took great pride in their heritage and ancestry and their respect for the aged was remarkable. Not far from the house on Guillaume Macau was a residence for the elderly and during my rotation in geriatrics, I would visit and be astonished at the cleanliness and congenial atmosphere. Many of the seniors had never seen a person of color, but most of them knew about the Congo and called me a Congolese. Because of their age and out of respect, I did not tell them any difference.

The exams were given again in October and unfortunately I failed a second time. During that summer, my husband had visited me and cut into my study time. He arranged for us to take a week away from the city and travel to Paris and Madrid. I had not been out of Brussels since my arrival in Europe and a chance to have a hiatus was welcomed. We arrived in Paris on July 13, 1953, the day before the Bastille Day holiday. The entire city was preparing for the holiday and it was all so very exciting. It was almost as if we were back in the States getting ready for a Fourth of July barbeque. We visited the Louvre, the Arc de Triumphe, and Le Mont Saint Michel and enjoyed an aperitif at a sidewalk café. The food was rich and exquisite and I must admit we ate a bit too much, but we were on vacation and I was not going to let anything or any worries cloud good times.

Our little girl took pictures of everything. Daddy Dear had brought a brownie camera for her and she made good use of it. Unfortunately, he took it back with him to have the photographs developed and we never got a chance to see them. On the sixteenth, we rode the train to Madrid, a beautiful and clean city, and unbelievably hospitable. My memory of our sightseeing tour is not as vivid as that of Paris and we only stayed for thirty-two hours, but we did enjoy the food, the music, and the Museo del Prado.

Upon our return and after Vincent's departure, I tried very hard to get back into the swing of things, but I had been too distracted by the visit and travel, so I repeated the course again the following year and failed again in June; thus leaving me only one more chance to pass or to be forced to withdraw from the university altogether. I gave it some serious thought. I went as far as to pack my books in the trunk. I notified my proprietors that I would probably be withdrawing and they were not pleased because of all of the time and effort I had put in. They tried to encourage me and even my daughter who had learned to express herself in French said, "Oh, woman, fait un efford!"—make the effort.

By this time I had begun to wonder if I had done the right thing by attempting a course of study in medicine at the age of forty-four, having completed college some twenty years prior. I had spent some time at Columbia University in New York City toward a master's degree with a credit of thirty-two points, but none directly related to medicine. I had forgotten a great deal of what I had learned and it took so much time for me to coordinate such a vast amount of material in the French language and then recite my exams to the professors. However, each time they said they could see an improvement in my presentation, so I took it all into consideration and decided to try again.

Then, several encouraging ideas came to mind, which added weight to my decision. A book that I read when I was a very young child in elementary school flashed into my mind. It was "Dick Whitaker and His Cat." I had not thought of that story for some time. An important sentence in the book was "Turn again, Whitaker, Lord Mayor of London." The story in short was that of an English lad by the name of Dick Whitaker who was hired to work in a kitchen somewhere in England and was under the supervision of a cruel task master. This man would always strike young Whitaker on the ears instead of advising him of what had to be done. The poor lad grew very tired and weary of this treatment and decided to run to get away from him. He took his cat with him and set out on his way not knowing where to go because he was an orphan and had no relatives. As he was crossing the London Bridge, he heard the sound of the bells of Big Ben which seemed to be saying, "Turn again, Whitaker, Lord Mayor of London." Dick repeated the sound, "Lord Mayor of London." This sound caused him to turn and go back to the kitchen of the King's palace and resume his employment. Not long after, the palace became overcome by rats and the King was told of the lad with a cat. He summoned Dick with his cat to rid the palace of the rats. The cat did so well that soon, all of the rodents were gone. The King was so pleased that he offered his daughter's hand to Dick and they were married. The King knighted Dick, Lord Mayor of London, and he and the Princess lived happily ever after.

The recollection of the story had a great impact on what had become a major decision-making time in my life. I was standing there at the tomb of the Unknown Soldier as I had done so many times before, thinking how this young person's life had been cut short while I had such a great opportunity ahead of me and I wanted to visit this place one last time before I left Belgium.

That evening I decided to stop at a theater and see a movie. I just had to have time to think. I cannot remember the title but the feature actress was Cyd Charisse and she was dancing and dancing and my attention was centered on the movement of her shoulder blade sliding up and down the thoracic cage. The thought came to me that I must learn more about that and coupled with the story of Dick Whitaker renewed inspiration came from somewhere and as I was preparing for the voyage home, a passage from the bible came to me clear and without provocation, "My Grace is sufficient for thee." So when the going had gotten rough, my faith had weakened. The scripture, Dick and his cat, and my intrigue to know more about the human body and my burning desire not to disappoint my friends and family and, most of all, my husband, whom I felt was making the ultimate immeasurable sacrifice in my behalf was a great factor in changing my mind. Invariably, I had found myself saying repeatedly, "I can't let Daddy Dear down; I can't let my husband down."

After making my final determination, I proceeded to unpack my books and clothes and started out with renewed courage to follow through with my original plan. When I told my husband of my plan to withdraw from the university, he failed to respond pro or con, thus leaving me to feel that he was displeased to know that I was about to abandon an idea that I had been so much in favor of doing.

My anatomy professor Dr. Dalque was at least tolerant with me at the beginning, but since I had failed some of my courses on two occasions, especially anatomy, he became less tolerant and finally made these remarks, "I advise you to go home and stop spending your husband's money. You will not succeed anyplace here in Europe because you don't have the mentality." I had also spoken to friends and classmates from the States who also felt that I was wasting my time because I would not accomplish anything. One of them was even in agreement with the professor and said, "You know, Hazel, I think Dr. Dalque is right. I have been helping you and you have shown no marked improvement." Stanley had been out of college for one year. I had graduated some twenty years prior to my entrance in medical school. His knowledge was at his fingertips and although I had a college degree, he, too, felt that I was not capable of pursuing a course in medicine.

But there were other faculty members who had a bit more compassion for me and at this point, I had no alternatives. I had to pass. It was my last chance to fail or be forced to withdraw from the school. All of my former classmates had passed to the third candidature and I was faced with all new people. To me these were happy-go-lucky young adults there to study but still playful in nature. I remember one incident in the anatomy lab when a young American who was dissecting the ear made a lewd remark and the professor dismissed him for the day. I never could get any of the other students to tell me exactly what was said, but I was told it had something to do with the female anatomy. The rules and code of ethics were strict, but our instructors received unfaltering respect. My experiences with the cadavers gave me an appreciation for those who donated their bodies so that we could study the organs and their function. I never could have imagined the inner workings of the muscles in relation to the bones and tendons nor would I have believed that the brain was so heavy in the hand. I was outstanding to those youngsters because not only was I a Negro woman, but I had reached the age of forty-six and I began when I was forty-four—the age of some of their parents.

The school year passed rapidly. Much of the material was a matter of review. Dr. Dalque became ill during the year and he was no longer in charge of the anatomy course, and so the exams were given by another professor. There was a sad story going around about Dr. Dalque's life, which made him bitter to female medical students for a long time, even his own daughters. I was told that he had only one son who became ill and was not able to complete his medical studies and this had dealt a hard blow to the father and it took a long time before he could face the defeat. I understand that since that time, however, he was able to face reality and began to consent for his daughters to study medicine. I had compassion for the old gentleman.

Upon completion of the second and third "candi", it began to be very exciting. The reading, speaking, and understanding of the French language had become clear to me. My courage and self-confidence had soared and I had no more fear of failing. At the end of every exam, there was a whisper around the university, "Did Madame Greene pass?" as though they expected the worse again but I did pass and all those who wished me well were elated to hear the good news and offered hearty congratulations. It was the first summer since my arrival in Belgium that I enjoyed a sense of freedom.

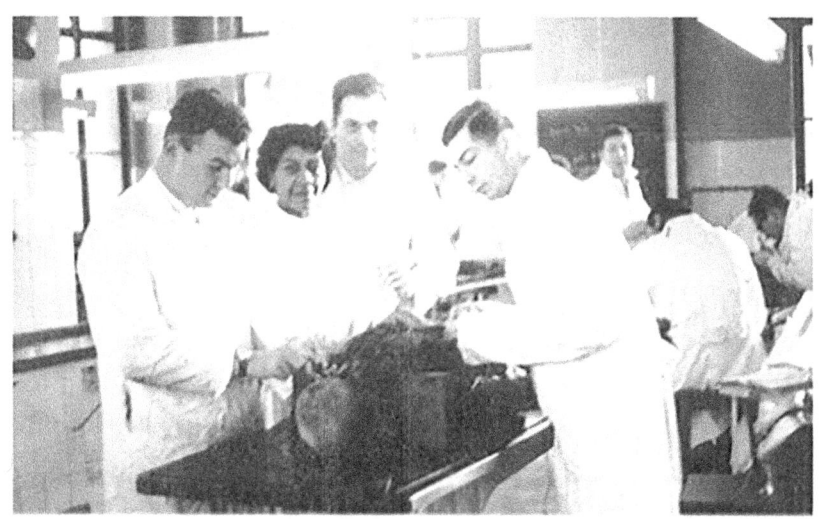

Anatomy class ULB, 1953

Chapter Five
The Doctoral Years

My daughter and I spent a lot of time getting reacquainted and acquainted with ourselves and our friends. We walked in Le Bois de la Cambre, admired Le Cinquantenaire and La Grande Place, strolled down La Rue Faussé aux Loups to deposit some money in our savings, and visited a few friends in the countryside. We also managed to move at this time to a modest apartment behind our current location. Being reared in close quarters had prepared me well for European standards which were old world and small compared to the United States.

Our new place was located on the third floor and there were only two toilets for the entire house. One was located in the bathroom of the proprietor, Monsieur Honoré Garnier, on the main floor and the other on the second, one flight down from our door. We did, however, have our own kitchen with running water and a small gas two-eye cooking outlet. The sitting room, which also served as a dining room, contained a wood-burning pot belly stove which heated the entire apartment and in front of which our weekly bath would be taken in a huge tin tub. The bedroom had two large beds, an armoire, and a dresser and my daughter decorated the walls with all sorts of class projects and movie star photographs. Each Sunday night, we would kneel at the foot of one of the beds and pray, "I would thank God for protecting us this far and I would ask for him to watch over our loved ones back home." We would recite together the 23rd, 24th, or 100th Psalm, sometimes all of them. I was thankful for each day that we were living and praying for accomplishment of our quest. I did not practice any specific religious belief but I taught my child to believe in God and to keep him in her heart wherever she goes and that God answers all prayers. That spring I enrolled her in a day camp for the summer and she spent two weeks in an overnight campsite in July.

The Université Libre de Bruxelles was founded in 1834 and was based on the scientific principal that one should engage in actions and words that he holds to be truth and have courage to defend his beliefs. Each year on Founder's Day, November 20, the university students would have a ceremony followed by a joyous parade from the school to downtown Brussels. The occasion was called "Jour des Etudiants," Students' Day. One year, I decided that I would participate in the festivities and walk with some of my classmates. Forgetting that they had youth on their side, I walked and sang for many kilometers to the center of the city. The weather was brisk and dry and the group was lively and encouraged by onlookers. Finally after several hours, I had to drop out and return by trolley. The next day, my aching bones reminded me that parades are for the youngsters, and that I should have stayed home, but I survived nevertheless with fond memories of the experience.

When I passed my first course of study, I sent letters to my husband, my family, and friends. Many sent acknowledgments and wished me continued success. My husband and in-laws were very encouraging and they, too, felt a little eager when my progress was slow. They were aware of what was involved in arriving in Belgium and starting out on a new adventure. It was actually the first milestone of a long way and there were many more to come, but it was at least a start. Many of my professors appeared elated at my progress. The registrar and his staff joined in wishing me continued success for the remainder of my journey. Dr. Cunningham was especially relieved because he was instrumental in helping me to enter ULB and get started in my medical studies. The apparent lethargy was beginning to cause him some anxieties; however, he was always encouraging me and helping me over the rough spots.

I remember one day I was reviewing the skull and what I was studying did not seem to make sense and the exams were a few days away. I asked him to come and help me in my review. Though he was busy he came over and helped me to clinch the main points. In the meantime, I was crying, but my crying did not faze him a bit.

He said "Women like to cry." So my crying spell cleared up and so did my mental state and I was able to have a rewarding review. My greatest concern was to get started on the first Doc. And I realized that it was necessary to begin with the intention of completing it in one year. This I did. I attended lectures regularly, took notes as well as I could, and spent time studying them. Le Mois de Bloc (Cram month) was the time allotted for a thorough review of the year's work and came as usual in May. The final exams were in June and the year of study was ended.

In the summer of 1955, my child and I once again had time together and I was able to attend the functions she participated in with the Girl Scouts and we would take a short train ride and visit some of our acquaintances in the countryside. I had arranged for her to go to camp with a classmate named Marie-Paule. The girl's mother made all of the arrangements. She even prearranged a train trip for the parents to visit while the children were there. I don't remember the name of the place but I arrived with so much stuff that Butchie said I looked like I was moving in. We were given a tour of the grounds and attended a skit in which my child was cast as Shenandoah, an Indian chief. Well, I guess so, I thought to myself. She was brown, had war paint on her face, and her hair was long and straight. Thank God she had not let them wash it. She would have been cast as Boola Boola, an African chief.

When she returned home while awaiting the beginning of the school year, she and her friends would go to the movies and stay for the film twice and, of course, when she came home, she felt obligated to tell me the whole story. Our arrangement was inconvenient sometime in that we shared the same room and very often when I was in a deep concentration, she would chirp out asking me if I wanted to hear a song or story she had learned during the day. That meant that I had to lay my work aside and listen to what she had to say and every moment of study, this summer was crucial because it was the summer study of the doctoral years. But, I was also concerned about my teenage daughter who was exhibiting the signs of being premenstrual and I had not yet had "that little talk" with her that every mother dreads. I asked her if she and her little friends talked about boys and if she knew about the menstrual cycle. She said, "Mommie, I know about bleeding," and she started to walk off. "Wait a minute," I said, "I have a few things to explain." I told her not to let any boy persuade her into the sex act by putting his penis between her legs. "Oh no," she said, "not with me, maybe the other girls do that, but not me!" She took me by surprise. I didn't know what to say. Months later, her cycle did show up and she simply showed it to me and asked if I had purchased any pads for her. I felt confident that she would be able to handle this transition. I told her not to discuss it with any of her friends, that it was a confidential matter, and that it would be over in a few days. But when I told her that it would happen again next month, she said, "What!" and "for how long, I thought it was a one time thing!" When I told her that she had 40+ years to go, she was stunned and irritated but shrugged it off. Until next month, I thought to myself.

In July we were invited by the LaMarque family to travel with them to Italy. Mrs. Martine LaMarque had met Butchie at La Ruche and thought that she was a remarkable young lady and wanted to meet her mother. Butchie had told her all about my studies and where we had traveled from, so her daughter Solange made sure that we would meet. We became friends instantly and she was so impressed with my endeavors. She, too, had wanted to return to school after her daughter was born but was discouraged by her husband. So twelve years into the marriage, she was now a full-time law student and very proud of it and her husband was fully supportive and sponsoring a getaway for his wife and daughter.

The four of us traveled by train to Milano by way of Paris, where we discovered antique shops, museums, and the architecture. We so wanted to get tickets to The Scala Theatre, but the immediate performances were sold out and I remember purchasing several yards of fine lace that I would tuck away for Butchie's wedding gown. I had never seen the art of tattering before and it was all so new to me and the lace was delicate and inexpensive. The following morning, we boarded our tour bus for the trip to Firenze. We were going to be in the city of the cradle of the Renaissance for two days. I was delighted. We were guided to the Galleria dell'Accademia Museum to see Michelangelo's David, to the Ponte Vecchio, and shopping in the Via de Calzaiuole where I purchased a beautiful white leather handbag for Butchie which I believe she still owns today.

We continued our travel and arrived in Venezia fairly early in the morning and bells were chiming in the Plaza San Marco softly but audible and those pigeons were everywhere. To me it was just as the stories I had heard when I was a girl in Berry O'Kelley except this time, I was right there taking it all in. I felt like a child again in wonderland with all of those birds. I wondered, so where do they go at night or do they sleep on the plaza? I should have gone back that evening to see for myself but I did not dare venture out after dark. We met a nice young man named Franco while we were there and he served as our personal guide. We did not speak Italian, but he spoke French and we got along quite nicely. He also spoke a little English. The girls thought he was cute and let him practice as much as he wanted to, although he was murdering the Queen's language. In the evening, Franco took us to all of the little out of the way sights that were not on the day tour and to some of the family night spots where there was no drinking and a little dancing. On one of our shopping tours, I purchased a lovely piece of blue Venetian glass that I kept for years until it got misplaced during my move from Delano village to Esplanade Gardens.

Next we traveled to Rome to visit the Vatican and the Coliseum. We visited the Sistine Chapel and gazed at La Pieta and the ceiling for a long time. "It must have taken that old man forever to accomplish such a task," Martine remarked. I was stunned by it all and amazed by the detail in the marble sculpture. In the city, we took pictures in front of the fountain and ate galati and a delicious bread, although I cannot recall its name.

It had taken me a little while to become accustomed to the Italian currency. I had never seen so many lira in exchange for a franc but the storekeepers were gracious and patient. If they cheated us, I never knew it but I did worry about it because my spending money was short. At night, I would lay awake thinking of the money I was spending and how I would have to ask Vincent to send a little extra when we returned, but I did not let that thought spoil our vacation, nor did I let my friend know that I was worried. We were having a wonderful time and I knew that this was an opportunity of a lifetime for Butchie and me both. I never told anyone back home that I had taken two weeks off to travel frivolously with my daughter. I didn't want it to get back to Vincent who believed that I had been toiling all summer.

Our last stop was Pisa. We were only there for an hour, just enough time to get souvenirs and take photographs of the tower and it was back on the bus to meet the train for our return home. On the way back, we asked God for a safe ride and thanked him for the new friendships. Some of the travelers were nuns whose sole purpose for the trip was to visit Vatican City; however, most of us were just tourists, we all prayed aloud and laughed together and sang.

As soon as we got back, I called the rooming house where Cunningham was staying to let him know that we were back. He said he would be over that very night. When he arrived, he was accompanied by fellow students Carl and Sydney both from New York, both seeking a medical degree from ULB. They were young men full of energy and spunk. They brought news from Harlem, rock and roll records by Bill Haley and the Comets, ginger snap cookies, and taught us how to dance the mash potatoes.

The States were beginning to seem far away now, but Providence would intervene once again. In September 1955, a young Negro student arrived in Belgium and somehow we became acquainted. His name is Ralph Thomas Mabry from Tallahassee, Florida. He had married Gwendolyn McCants, a charming southern girl from Mobile, Alabama, and together they had two lovely children and one on the way. They had met at City College of New York and his lifelong dream was to become a physician. They were a great couple and immediately they became family. I've always said that one is born with relatives, but one chooses family. They were living in a small apartment on Rue des Tanneurs near the University, but it quickly became too small when their third child arrived in February. I remember helping Ralph get Tommy, 5, and Linda, 4, dressed to go to the Hospital St. Pierre to see their new sister, Maggie. On the way there, he told me the story of the delivery and how when the baby emerged the obstetrician, who had never delivered a Negro baby before, held the newborn in his hands and inquired, "Monsieur, est-vous satisfait?" (Sir, are you satisfied?) apparently not aware that our babies are often born very pink in color. Ralph pointed to the child's cuticles and told him this would probably be her permanent skin tone and that he was very satisfied.

Shortly thereafter, they moved to the upstairs of the Wasson family home and settled in very quietly. Many times, we would study together and Butchie would help Gwen by playing with Tommy and Linda so she could cook and care for the baby. They all were so fascinated because Gwen was breastfeeding and they laughed because Maggie seemed so greedy. I remember once they asked to taste the breast milk and nearly gagged. They could not understand how the baby thought it was so good. Butchie said it tasted like carrot juice. I wondered where she had had a chance to taste carrot juice before.

Madame Wasson was a gracious woman whose husband worked in the Congo. Their daughter Claudine was a teenager who was intrigued by people of color, especially Americans, and practiced speaking English as much as possible. She would hang around upstairs talking with Gwen and playing with Maggie and once made the remark that she thought Ralph was the most handsome man she had ever met. She attended the Lycee de St. Gilles, an excellent high school, and in years to come, I would enroll my daughter there.

There was a considerable change in the program that year. There was an addition of courses and a continuation of some of the old ones, plus daily hospital rounds in the morning, courses in the evening, and on-call duty one night per week. There was a great increase in responsibility and quite a contrast to the candidatures and I had to be so very mindful of my child's everyday activities. I was so thankful that I had friends with whom she could spend the night and still get to school the next day.

My first night on-call, I was working with one of my coworkers, Francois Débauche. It was all so new for the both of us, but we were under the supervision of an upperclassman who directed us both as to what to do. There was the duty of taking blood pressure, temperature, and giving medication. One particular patient had been in an automobile accident and was badly battered. There was swelling of the face, head, upper and lower extremities with the presence of numerous hematomas (an accumulation of blood under the skin), and whose vital functions had to be monitored throughout the night.

There was an "on-call" room for the male doctors, but there were no special provisions made for females who had to share the room with the males and this was new to me. So I removed my hospital coat and slept in my clothes. This was uncomfortable but tolerable. We were also given a half day off the day following the "on-call" night which we utilized to attend classes and get some sleep if needed.

My first externship was done at Brugman Hospital in the medical ward. There I began to do clinical work. The duties consisted of drawing blood for necessary tests, physical examinations, general admission and discharging, and daily rounds with the doctor in charge in order to acquaint ourselves with illness and treatments. We were at liberty to ask questions and the doctor had the same privilege. I spent a great deal of time in the surgical unit because being the only black female and at an age far advanced from my classmates, they were able to choose assignments ahead of me and on many occasions, I got stuck with the leftovers which put me on the surgical ward many times. However, I felt privileged. I gained a great deal of knowledge and experience just by being present, but my chances for scrubbing up for surgery were not as numerous as they should have been and I remember my first experience. A doctor came in and wanted someone to assist in a chipped bone repair. He saw me and said, "Have you ever scrubbed for surgery?" I lied and said, "Yes." He said, "Scrub up!" It was not a major event but it was my chance to go through the act. The nurse in charge was not very cordial and made no attempt to help the situation. Shortly thereafter, she was assisting in a gall bladder procedure and I was there as an observing resident. The doctor meticulously completed the surgery and attached the drainage tube but found it to be nonfunctional. He removed the tube and threw it halfway across the floor and gave the nurse "Hell!" She was so humble and apologetic. I am sure that she remembered her hostile actions towards me and after that, she acted more amicably and gave me consideration as a medical student.

During the time that I was doing part of my training as I would come to the end of my bus ride, there was a lane that led to the hospital that was lined with pear trees and during the season, huge fruits could fall on the ground. On my way back, I would fill my briefcase with those pears, take them home, and make several jars of pear preserves. It was a deviation from my studies and a mind-freeing experience. Some of them I kept and gave to my friends when I arrived back in the States.

The first doctoral year was a success and at the end of the school year, my Butchie and I did many things that we wanted to do during the year, some of which included visiting museums, parks, the botanical gardens, libraries, the symphony orchestra, and many other points of interest.

My next year of study was the second doctorate and much of my time was spent in two hospitals, St. Gilles and Anderlecht. My experiences were quite fruitful there as well as many classes in pathology, cardiology, internal medicine, pediatrics, and Obs/Gyn. The courses were beginning to intensify at this point and the pressure was on. I remember helping with a delivery. The physician on-call asked if I had ever actually been in the field, a term used for the obstetrician's location when a patient is about to give birth. I nodded, so he asked me to assist and since I had already scrubbed, he put me in position carefully showing me how not to have my face too close. But just at that moment, the patient gave a big push, out came the baby's head right into my hands and the one shoulder and the next and a lot of stuff gushed right into my face. Luckily the nurse was there to wipe my eyes so I could continue.

In November, Gwen and I decided that we should have a genuine Thanksgiving dinner with all of the trimmings. This was my first since 1951. I remember starting the night before and roasting a fifteen- to twenty-pound turkey in a coal stove for fourteen hours. Between sleeping and studying, I would open the stove belly door and baste the bird with the drippings every hour or so. At their place, Gwen must have been chopping, dicing, and mixing because on Thanksgiving day, we had an excellent meal. We arrived with the turkey, a coconut cake, and green beans seasoned with fat pork meat to add to the carrots, mashed potatoes with chopped leek greens, baked apples, steamed leek stems wrapped in bacon with white sauce, and chocolate cake Gwen had prepared. We prayed that we would survive our ordeal and return home soon; this the first American holiday I had celebrated since I left home.

During the winter season, most of my time was spent studying. My child was safe when she was visiting the Mabry's or at "La Ruche" so I did not have to worry about her too much. We would spend a minimum amount of time together. We would shop, play Canasta, a card game the Charleteaux couple had taught us, and sit by the lake.

One day traveling back from one of our excursions on the way to Porte de Namur where we would have to transfer, an incident happened that I must tell. I had been teaching my daughter respect for others, the elderly and me, such as holding the door for someone, getting up to allow an older person to sit down, and helping me with the grocery bags or getting out of a taxi. We were laughing, talking, and making plans for dinner when we arrived at our transfer location. The doors opened and Butchie jumped off the trolley and headed down the street. After a few steps, she realized that I was not behind her and looked over her shoulder. There I was standing in the doorway of the exit hanging by one hand waiting for her to help me down the last step. She hurriedly came back, extended her hand, and helped me down. The people seated in the tram were amused and laughing. Butchie was embarrassed, but I hugged her and walked to our next ride vowing never to forget the incident.

Then came the news that Daddy Dear was arriving from Paris. I was delighted so much so that I did not even stop to realize that I had not even been aware of his intentions to travel to Europe. At first I was regretful that our daughter, who was away at summer camp, would not get a chance to see her father, but when he actually arrived, I found out the real reason for his visit. Vincent had decided that he wanted a divorce and no longer wanted to wait for my return to the U.S. He had papers and all and as I read and read, I realized that in the settlement he was willing to pay child support until Lillie was eighteen as well as set up a trust fund for her until the age of twenty-one as well as pay for my medical studies until I finished and sponsor our return trip to New York. I was in tears. After all, I loved my husband and thought all along that I was doing all of this for the both of us, but looking back on all of it, I now understand that it must have been tough on a man in his mid-forties to live alone and have all of his friends and family taunt him and have to face the humiliation of being called Dr. Greene's husband.

    Reluctantly I signed the papers giving Vincent his freedom and trusting God that all would go as indicated. At this point I had decided not to let anything stand in the way of what I wanted to accomplish. Years later, I found out the divorce situation had been orchestrated by a woman he later married and who, in fact, had traveled with him and was waiting in Paris for him to return with the signed agreement.

    After Vincent left, I was quite distort. I started walking up the Chausée d'Ixelles toward town. It was a good way for me to think and decide what I was going to say to "Butchie." I stopped in a department store to look around without any specific item in mind. I must have stayed in the store no longer than twenty minutes. As I was leaving, I was stopped by a smartly dressed young woman who identified herself as a store detective. She stated that she had observed me shoplifting and she showed me her credentials. She asked me to step back and precede her to the office. I was baffled and not wanting to cause a scene I walked quietly in front of her as she directed me to the rear. Once in the office, she and two men began telling me how serious the charges were and that I would have to be searched for stolen items. I ardently protested and denied taking anything from the store without paying. In fact, I said that I had not made a purchase at all. The lady stated that she saw me put my hand in my pocket in the accessories department and that I must have had something in my palm. I showed them my handkerchief that contained several bills and coins that Vincent had given me prior to his departure and my passport and I said, "See, I have money, why would I be in here stealing?" Nevertheless, I was escorted to a small cubicle and strip-searched by a second woman who had entered the room. I was so humiliated. Something like this had never happened to me. I started crying but my tears were ignored and I was also afraid since I was a black woman alone without witnesses and they could injure me and I would have no recourse. During the search, they did not find a thing belonging to the store because I had not taken anything, so the case was dropped and I was told never to come back. A police van was called to drive me home and I was let out several blocks from our house as not to cause me any embarrassment in the neighborhood, but I was embarrassed and humiliated. The divorce papers were hurtful enough, but this incident made me feel even worse.

That summer, the long days of study turned into nights and many times I saw dawn, but in spite of it all, in September I did not receive a passing grade. In October 1957, I repeated the second doctorate without incident. All of the material was so familiar to me and this time, I was able to apply myself without distractions. I enrolled my daughter in a more aggressive lycee in St. Gilles. This school would offer her studies in Latin, humanities, and science, necessary for matriculation to college upon our return to the United States. The issues of Little Rock, Arkansas, had reached us in Europe and several persons had stopped us on the street to ask my opinion on the subject. One woman said, "We don't have that sort of thing here, do we?" I told her it was because there was not an abundance of people of color here. Prejudice follows wherever one goes. I had experienced it as a child in the south, again when I wanted to go to medical school, and now I had to face the stares and glares of the Belgian people who wanted to know why our hair was straight and not kinky like the Congolese they had read about. They adored King Léopold and did not know of the atrocities done in the Congo. They just knew that Belgium owned the land and its people. I chose this school for its curriculum and for the proximity to home and the hospital where I worked. I made sure that she had adequate clothing to last throughout the school year although the school had a uniform requirement, but she had to have shoes and she was already wearing a size 41 (ladies 10 U.S.) and we struggled to find girlish styles in that size. I remember once suggesting that she wear a pair of mine to a school function and she replied that she did not want to wear "old lady shoes." Of course Gwen was there to help me and our relationship helped us through the last months of our stay in Europe. Even after their return, we remained close and even today she, her husband, and children call me Auntie Hazel.

Once again my studies went uneventfully since the entire year was a review. Nevertheless, I put in some long hours of study as well as many hours in the hospitals. I also made time to attend academic and scout functions Butchie participated in.

We lived very modestly and economically now. Vincent kept the money coming as promised, but it was barely enough to pay rent, buy food and a few necessities here and there. Many times I would go to the farmers' market on the square and go behind the booths and pick up discarded turnip and cauliflower leaves, then purchase a strip of fat back pork meat, and cook up a mess of greens. Once my child said, "Mother, François, one of my friends, whose family sold vegetables at the market, said 'I saw your mother picking up food behind the stands.'" I asked her what her reply was. She said she shrugged her shoulders and remarked, "So we eat good leaves you throw away or give to your rabbits!" She knew that one day, we would be returning to the United States and that life would be very different and affluent then. I never hid her parentage nor did I accept a defeatist attitude from her. She had been blessed with the opportunity to be Hazel and Vincent's daughter and I gave her all of the love and compassion I never received as a child.

By the time the school year ended, I had already made preparations for summer camp and in her absence, I would study for the upcoming exams. That summer, the long awaited 1958 World's Fair opened in Brussels. My daughter was thrilled. I managed to squeeze enough money out of our slim budget to get a long-term entry pass which would allow her access to all of the display pavilions every day.

I struggled a lot with my studies that summer, especially since I did not have much time for her during those months and I thank God that she was a respectful, obedient, and calm child who managed quite well on her own. There were times when she was defiant and rebellious, typically a teenager and she had lots of friends who were much older than she was, but her appearance deceived them into believing that she is one of their peers. She was tall, slender, and had good legs. Her hair was also quite long. I spent hours combing it. She no longer liked to wear braids. Heck, Mother made us wear braids until we were sixteen. I remember one time when I had to take time from my studies to go to the police station to confirm her age. It seems that she and a few other kids were going to a pub that was off limits to children and of course "Butchie," who was as developed as a seventeen-year-old wanted to go somewhere to dance and listen to music. I had to show her ID card as well as our passports and sign a sworn statement acknowledging that the location was off limits to minors. I had no idea that they served beer there.

During that time she had risen in rank at "La Ruche" and many of her activities kept her quite busy supervising other children during the summer camp and two-week tours and hikes to the mountains in neighboring countries. These activities gave her exposure to many cultural advantages as well as allowing me time to concentrate on my work even more.

October 1958 marked the beginning of the clinical year. This meant that very few hours were spent in class while most of my days and several nights would be in practice on the hospital wards. The entire year went by very quickly. This was the time when I learned what responsibility for human wellness was all about. My child stayed with the Mabry's in a neighboring section of town but close enough to allow her to attend the same school, see her friends, as well as the scouting activities. During the Christmas holidays, she visited The Netherlands and Luxembourg with the Vrooman Family and had a great vacation. I did not spend a lot of time with her. I did not cook a balanced meal every night nor did I have a chance to teach her how to do so. Somehow, though, we managed to remain healthy except for a gnawing pain in my stomach from the anxiety of study; yet somehow she profited from all of her acquaintances by learning the art of baking and drawing, neither of which I could do well.

After the New Year, time seemed to go by very swiftly. Spring was here once again and I was ready for a deeper focus into some of those phases of medical study reserved for the upperclassmen. This year would mark my eight year of medical studies, a course that would have taken me only four in an American school, but I was not bitter. It was time well spent and the education my daughter received would always be with her. Upon entry to the fourth doctoral, all students had to present and defend in front of a medical jury a thesis based on his or her personal experience. This had to be from your general medicine or biochemical research. The course consisted of thirty hours of medical statistics; 285 hours of general medicine comprising of social medicine, hygiene, radiology, medical law, and gerontology; and 270 hours of clinical practice at Brugman Hospital including the on-call nights.

I remember using my study time very wisely and having few leisure moments with my child and it troubled me a great deal. On rare occasions, we would walk in the Bois de la Cambre, a scenic woodsy area of town, and admire God's handiwork. The trees would remind me of the farm back home and the loveliness of it all. We would walk from our front door to the Porte de Namur, a shopping area in town, and browse in Le Bon Marché, a variety store, for a half hour. Occasionally we would take in a movie, especially when it was American made and in English, and read the French subtitles.

This was the summer that La Ruche had planned a two-week trip in Bavaria for the leaders and of course, Butchie was eligible to go. Apparently, without my knowledge, she had studied and passed an examination which would allow her to advance to a higher level from team to troop leader and although she was always so enthusiastic about such events, I always felt a little guilt about sending her off somewhere so I could study. Previously she had traveled with her team for a week, but now she would be gone for fifteen days. I reminded her to make the best of it because I was hoping that the following summer a whole new kind of experience would unfold.

I hired a taxi and we rode up Chausée d'Ixelles to meet the bus and load the duffel bags and suitcases. The young ladies were glad to see her as usual, but this time was different as if somehow it was known that this probably would be her last time with them. When the bus departed, I stood there for a few moments with a heavy heart, then I walked back to the apartment to resume my studies. Two weeks later when she returned, it was with many photographs, new songs, and scratched legs. Apparently it was supposed to be a sign of a good hiking experience in the deep woods. Luckily they were superficial and not on her face. She told me many stories, details of the trip, and a dozen German phrases she had learned in the little village where they were boarded. I could tell that she had had a wonderful time and the memories would stay with her forever.

Hazel Coley-Greene

Medical students Hazel and Louis L'Agneau

Brugman Hospital, 1959

Chapter Six
The Beginning of the End

Hopefully, this was going to be our last Christmas in Brussels and eight long years of study had taken their toll. I was still considering myself a young woman in spite of my age. I believe age is a state of mind over the chronological order of things, but still, I had to go back home a divorcee now with a child in tow, find a place to live, get a job, and pass the New York Medical Boards. I sent letters of introduction to several hospitals in the metropolitan New York area, but I hoped for a position at Harlem, the hospital of the community that I had left. I knew I would be starting at a very low salary, but with several years of child support ahead of me, I knew I would be able to manage with Vincent's help. Usually, hospitals offered staff intern and residents lodging if needed and I was told such arrangements could be made for females through the School of Nursing.

As usual, we did not have an elaborate holiday season but Butchie was in a play at La Ruche which I attended. She as quite good on stage or was it just a mother's pride? We received several invitations to visit from friends as well as the Mabry's and we managed to accept them all and spend many hours of joy together. Gwen and I baked chocolate and coconut cakes, fried chicken, and squeezed dozens of lemons to make a beverage. The Débauche family treated us to provincial cuisine and chicory coffee and our other friends made us feel welcomed in their homes.

By Easter, Vincent had already made the travel arrangements and sent the tickets for our transatlantic voyage home. Our ship was "La Liberté," and once again, we would be traveling by train to Paris to catch the boat in Cherburg. So it was spring again, April 1960. I was very busy with studies and on-call nights and the pressure of the everyday struggle to survive was taking its toll and I was in ill health. During the mois de block, I rarely left the apartment and ate very little and constant stomach pains hindered my progress. Nevertheless, I struggled to take the exams. Midway I was hospitalized with a bleeding ulcer and Dr. Jean Pasteels came to my bedside to administer the oral exam to me. The floor staff had been very supportive and the nurses often sat in with me while I was reviewing the material. I passed all of the exams and could finally feel that I had accomplished something and could see the light at the end of the tunnel.

I called my daughter, who had been staying with her best friend Muriel, the Rucquoy family, to bring some dress clothes so that I could attend the graduation ceremonies. She did and I was wheeled to the services in a chair because my attending physician would not release me. When my name was called, the audience of students and professors stood and applauded and many shook my hands, so much so that they were sore for several days.

The following month, a week prior to our departure, Butchie and I went shopping. She was a young lady now and I knew there were a few items of clothing that she would need while onboard the ship.

Our first stop was a boutique called Ann de Parmes where she chose a lovely blue two-piece dress that she kept for several years. Then we walked to l'Innovation, a department store nearby, for underwear and a cute white lace dress she felt she could not live without. Fortunately we did not have to purchase shoes because she had plenty of ballerinas which were popular at the time.

This last week of our sojourn in Europe was filled with excitement, anxiety, and anticipation. I had not lived in the U.S. for eight years and was going back to live on my own without anyone's support. My relatives had not been in favor of my decision to leave all that was known to me and pursue a career in medicine. How would they react to my return, although successful?

Medical Degree from ULB, July 6, 1960

Madame Le Docteur, Hazel Coley-Greene

On our final day in Brussels, we finished packing the few clothes that we had and since the apartment had already been furnished, we made sure it was clean and neatly arranged. We said good-bye to Monsieur Garnier and boarded a rented van for the Gare du Midi train station. After paying the fare and purchasing the tickets to Paris, I realized that we would not have enough money for the last leg of our journey and with my emotions on edge, tears came to my eyes. My child questioned me and had the idea to hop on the trolley and go back to our neighborhood and borrow some money from our friendly grocery store. While she was gone, I phoned Paul Fabo, a businessman from the Congo who had befriended us some years ago. He quickly came to the station and arrived just as my daughter was returning. With the money borrowed from him and from our neighbor, I felt safe that we would arrive in New York without incident. I assured him that he would be repaid and it must have been on faith alone that the man in the grocery store gave my child money knowing that we were traveling back to the States and that he might never hear from us again. God was so good to us. I repaid them both within a month.

Our train ride to Paris was pretty uneventful. We made the acquaintance with an American couple, the Ingersolls, and their children who had been touring Europe for the summer. We exchanged experiences, laughed a lot, and the youngsters got along well. By the time we reached Paris, we were both so tired that the prospect of checking in the hotel and getting a good night sleep was welcomed.

The next morning, we decided to take a walk to a nearby sidewalk café and have a light breakfast French style and it was lovely. We were not rushed and the weather was warm and we had plenty of time to catch the boat train. As we made our way back to the hotel, we glanced at a few fashions in shop windows and a sidewalk vendor gave my girl a flower. "Pour les cheveux," he said (for your hair).

As we arrived at the embarkation station, we were met by officers of the registry who asked to see our credentials. We were advised that our passport would expire on August 31, 1960, four days prior to our arrival in the port of New York and that we might be refused entry into the United States. As I was pondering what to do next;

I was told that another passenger and her child faced the same dilemma and that we would be taken to the United States Embassy and our credentials could be extended. We all were chauffeured there in a hurry and upon our return, the gangplank was removed and we set sail. The lady and her child were first-class passengers and Caucasian. I often wondered what would have happened to us if she had not been in the same situation. We finally found our way to our cabin. It was smaller than the one we had on our trip over, but I felt safe and happy that we had made it this far and we had each other, so we settled down to the first leisure time I had had in a decade.

The next few days were quite enjoyable. The afternoons were spent participating in onboard activities and in the evening, there would be dancing on the ballroom deck. My daughter was young, spry, and knowledgeable of all the latest steps, including the waltz, and the gentlemen passengers would line up to dance with her. I got such a kick out of seeing her have such fun. I remember advising her not to eat too greedily at the dinner hour because our money was scarce and she quickly reminded me that our meals were included in the fare. Boy, was I relieved for the oversight on my part. Imagine trying to curb a young teen's appetite. This time around, the food had a French flair and the meals were exquisite and I had no difficulty reading the menu, which was astonishing to our table companions who were U.S. citizens. Many passengers in the tourist class were students returning from overseas study or travel and there were also honeymooners, but there were only three females of color as far as I could tell and the other one was a young medical student that I had met in Brussels in the spring.

Many times I would stand on deck and watch the water move as we sailed and wondered who would be waiting for me when I reached home. I had notified my brother Ronald that I would not be expected to present myself for work right away and he said he would drive up to New York. I had also written to Gertrude Lowe and Leslie Ashby, two of my dear friends from the Dunbar who were there when we sailed eight long years ago. Gertie had invited us to stay with her until Ronald arrived from North Carolina and I graciously accepted. I was anxious to see everyone and to be safe at home in American territory again. The night before our arrival, there was a very lively party in the tourist class, so much so that even some of the first class passengers came in to enjoy the ambiance. I stayed there a short while. My daughter did not attend at all. She said she was too tired from all of the previous nights of dancing. In the morning, we moved very slowly passing Ms. Liberty. I made it a point not to miss her this time. Heck, I was one of Emma Lazarus' tired and poor, yearning to breathe free, and I was glad to be home again. I had promised to go south with my brother to visit the home farm and to reacquaint myself with some long lost relatives and to get some rest, so I was looking forward to that also.

I wanted to see my father's grave and make a visit to Dillard and Shaw. I also wanted to walk on the dirt where it all had begun and I did. I even picked up a few leaves and pecan shells and soil to feel it in my hand. While I was in Raleigh, I looked up some old acquaintances who told me that Alfreda Hill Carey was living in New York and that I should contact her. It would be wonderful, I thought to myself, to see her again, my childhood friend from school, and I decided that I would do so as soon as I got back home.

We returned from North Carolina shortly before Labor Day in time for me to secure lodging and enroll my child in school. Vincent still lived at 2588 Seventh Avenue in the Dunbar and since she would be living with him for the time being, he chose to register her in Washington Irving High School for girls because she had become accustomed to single gender classes in Europe. The school was located in lower Manhattan and our child would have to commute via subway. I was really concerned but Vincent said she would be okay since his stepdaughter would be attending the same school and would show her the ropes. I went along with the deal but somewhere in the back of my mind, I knew that soon I would make other arrangements.

Living in the nurses' residence was very easy for me and very convenient. After a long day on the wards, I could walk through the under tunnel and reach my room within minutes. I could eat in the hospital cafeteria or bring meals back for later consumption. There was a cleaning lady who would come around in the morning and collect any tableware left in the hallway. My neighbor was Dr. Chung

Yul Kwon, a lovely Korean-American woman who was finishing her residency in OB-GYN. From time to time, her husband would bring their young son Michael to visit and have dinner with her. He would bring Korean food and chopsticks and he even taught Butchie to use them one evening when she was visiting. Sometimes Dr. Kwon would stop by my room and recant amusing stories about her ancestors and we would laugh and laugh. Once a week, our hospital whites would be picked up and laundered. The skirts and jackets were made of heavy duty cotton and would come back starched to the max, so much so that they could stand up on their own, but we were happy to have the service.

Life in the residence was comfortable and my interaction with the students was rare, but occasionally, I would meet a student from a faraway state who had come to New York seeking a degree from the renowned Harlem Hospital School of Nursing. The school was fashioned as any college campus, all in one building. There was a classroom floor, a recreation room with games and television, a library, study rooms, administration office, and of course, sitting rooms; and the main doors were locked at 11 PM sharp. Once, the downstairs desk called to let me know that Butchie had two gentlemen callers, one sitting in each room on the west side. I advised the young woman that she was not in the building and that I would be down shortly. Fortunately, I knew the young men, so I spoke to them both and went back upstairs. It was at this point that I realized that I had to find a suitable place of residence for us to call home so that we could have company like normal folk since she did not invite anyone to Vincent's place.

I was beginning my rotations in October. I remember walking by Harlem years ago and saying to myself, someday I will be working here. Harlem is a good hospital affiliated with Columbia Presbyterian, a teaching institution of the New York City Health & Hospital Corporation. The opportunities for exposure, to all sorts of wounds, illness, and surgical procedures were endless. Harlem would be my working base while months of study were still ahead toward the New York State Board exams. I had become accustomed to cramming, so getting ready for the State Boards was just a continuation of my student days in Belgium, only this time the review was in my native language.

My daughter was a teen in high school now. Her European education had prepared her well and she was placed two grades ahead of her peers. Many of the courses she had studied in elementary school such as Latin, geometry, geography, and ancient history were being taught high school junior year. She had to double up on English classes, but her reading skills were excellent. I anticipated her having some problems only being able to use the metric system, but she adjusted quite well. Even living with Vincent and his new family went well. She was savoring the life of a typical American girl. She was going to church, having parties, and sightseeing around Manhattan Island.

Sometimes she would come by the hospital and have a meal with me but it was difficult because she never wanted to leave and the separation was painful. I missed being a part of her everyday activities and as she was matured I knew I would have to provide a better situation for the both of us. From time to time, Vincent would allow her to stay overnight with me at the School of Nursing but the room was small and only one of us could occupy the bed at a time. This arrangement was good during the nights when I was on-call, but many times, we were in there together and it was a calamity.

Finally, I was able to get a larger room and move her in completely. She and Vincent had a misunderstanding and living with him was no longer suitable for her. She skipped school one morning and came over to Harlem to speak with me about it. She looked real sad, but I told her that we would manage as we always had in the past, but there was still only one bed in my quarters. I spoke with one of the janitors who found a discarded mattress in a storage room downstairs and we hauled it to the room, cleaned it very well, and set it up like a trundle under my bed. She was a happy girl that day. Of course, the switchboard operator would have to interrupt her endless conversations to page me to the wards, but she was happy and so was I. Anyway, she was beginning to receive acceptance letters from colleges and universities, so I knew the arrangement would be of short duration.

It was during this time that I noticed a small area on my left leg that was swollen, tender, and warm. I dismissed it as an insect bite and continued my daily routine. After a few days, with closer examination, I realized that the reddened patch had grown in size and was quite painful and that I should let someone take a look. I mentioned the possibility of cellulitis to the chief of medicine during a meal in the cafeteria and he immediately made preparations for me to be admitted to the staff section of the hospital. Cellulitis, an inflammation of the subcutaneous tissue. Now how did I manage to get that? I was hospitalized for a week and every day, my daughter would come up for a visit, sometimes twice a day and sometimes she would fall asleep at my bedside. It must have been real lonely for her over there in the residence and a bit scary too.

In the summer of 1962, Gwen and the children returned to the States. Ralph was not with them. It seems that at the last minute, one of the professors did not give him a passing grade and he would have to take the class again. Upon his return, he would join me at Harlem Hospital and together we would study for the boards and look back and laugh at our time in Belgium. Gwen enrolled the children in a French-speaking school to being in the fall and I decided that it was time for my daughter to travel in her own country and experience her homeland as she had done with so many European territories. I was trying in every way to make her a well-rounded young woman and continue expanding her education by land travel to California. We would have the experience of seeing many places as well as visiting my relatives who had migrated to Los Angeles County while I was overseas.

I also wanted to see my mother's grave site. She had passed away in 1959 at the age of eighty. It had been a hurtful feeling for me not to have been there for her. After all, I loved my mother. The memories of her mothering me were not the best. I always felt that she was ashamed of me and consequently made me ashamed of my femininity. She had always wanted boys to work in the field and I think a girl represented competition for my father's affection. I never liked the way my mother treated me as a child, although it was not all bad, but I did not have the best of memories.

So we set out to cross the United States by Greyhound bus, a trip that Butchie did not welcome at all. She was out of school for the summer and wanted to frolic about New York City, Staten Island, and Palisades Park with her friend Nelda. Nevertheless, I tried to make her envision the fun and experiences we would have on such an adventure but to no avail.

On our trek westward, one of our major stops was in Chicago. This would be my first time there. I had read so much about the place. I hoped we would get a chance to walk in the city. The driver, however, announced that this was only a meal stop and there would be no time to leave the terminal. The platform was busy and the terminal was a crowded place, so we hurriedly went to the restrooms with an overnight bag to wash up and change clothes. Much to my surprise, there is a larger stall with shower and dressing area and it was vacant, clean, and ready for use. Feeling refreshed, we walked together to find the eating area and I chose the first little place we saw. We sat at the counter and looked at the menu when suddenly my daughter excused herself and left the table. After what seemed to me a long enough absence, I became concerned as any parent would of a teenager with crazy hormones and decided to look for her. A few shops down, she was sitting at a counter eating and talking with the waitress. I asked her why did she leave me at the other place and not tell me that she wanted to eat somewhere else. She just said, "I don't know," a typical teenage answer. I felt a bit hurt. In fact, I was quite peeved and with tears in my eyes I told her that we had been through a lot together and that all we truly had was each other and for her to just walk off without considering my feelings were hurtful. "We are a team," I said; we have endured too much to be at odds now. I don't know if the true understanding of what I was saying reached her because all she would express was her displeasure of leaving her friends at such an important time of her life. It was not until we returned that she found out that her friends did not miss her that much at all because fun goes on regardless of her presence.

We arrived in Los Angeles, California on August 7, 1962, the day Marilyn Monroe died. The talk of it was everywhere and for the next few days, it seemed that the entire nation was fascinated with her death. It almost was as if they had known her personally! It was during this time that Lillie got to know who her father really was, a strong-minded gentle man who loved life, his family, his dogs, and could bake the best chocolate cake with pecans on the frosting.

He talked with her for hours and for many days. He told her of her parentage, of how she came into being, the love he had for her and the pride he felt knowing he had at least a small part in the making of who she was. I believe the experience was a turning point in our relationship. She started to show an acknowledgment of how lucky she had actually been. Emmett had advised her to look for Alice, her birth mother, and hear her side of the story and to be fully armed with the truth of it all. He told her that this awareness would make her a strong woman, able to withstand any adversities, and that his love for her had enabled him to send her away with his sister. After a month-long visit with my relatives, trips to Disneyland, Knox Berry Farm, the beach, shopping on Hollywood Boulevard, and sightseeing tours, we flew back to New York on Pan American Airlines in preparation for school and the state boards.

In September 1962, I traveled to Greensboro, North Carolina, to enroll my daughter in school—Bennett College, a UNCF Methodist college for young women—where I knew she would receive an outstanding education. It had been her choice. She had also been accepted in many other schools in the United States as well as Canada, but we had relatives in Greensboro—Nell and Buddy Coley—and in the event she needed assistance, they would be there for her.

Upon our arrival at Barge Hall, the freshman dorm, we met Marsha Bullock, her roommate, a lovely young woman from California, a doctor's daughter who was poised and very friendly and the three of us decorated the room in green and yellow. Marsha also had a relative in Greensboro, her Aunt Mabel, who lived not far from the campus and I was happy to know that the girls could go there to get away from campus for a few hours. The college had many activities and formalities for the incoming young ladies and their parents and we attended them all. It was such a lovely quadrangle bordered with magnolia trees leading up to the chapel and the Bennett Bell. I reminisced to my days at Shaw University and I was nostalgic for the songs, the cheers, my classmates, and friends.

Chapter Seven

A Dream Realized

My trip back to New York was a lonely one. This was the first time in almost sixteen years that we would be separated for such a long period of time, but it felt right. She was quite a young lady and I had a feeling of joy at the prospects of her impending womanhood. I still had much work to do. I was beginning to feel every bit of my fifty-four years. Only God knew how many years lay ahead and how many I would be allowed to enjoy the gift of medical practice. I called Alfreda and she reassured me that everything will be okay. I told her that I knew it, but I just felt a bit sad.

After a few weeks, life began to settle into a routine of hospital work and study. Neither was foreign to me. The circumstances were just different. I was healing my people, they were teaching me, and my pride as a physician was soaring. I had dreamed many years of this opportunity and now here I am, Dr. Greene, a servant of the Harlem community. The hospital emergency room was a busy place on Friday and Saturday night, but it was my chance to see wounds of all types. My rotation in psychiatry proved to be quite a challenge, considering each resident was required to meet with the head of the department to discuss his or her state of mind on frequent occasions. I seemed to be doing well although I had many concerns about my teenager and dating. He advised me to take it in stride as long as the scholastic grades were up to par. I took the advice, finished my tour, and moved on to internal medicine.

During the annual staff Christmas party, I finally got a chance to speak with Dr. Harold Brooks, the chief of medicine. He was circulating on the dance floor and introducing his bride Marie. "Ah, Dr. Greene, I finally get a chance to shake your hand. I've seen you many times in the dining room and this is indeed a pleasure." On the floor Dr. Brooks immediately took me under his wing. He had a knack for communication with the patients and staff. He would move about the wards like one would do at home. In fact, he was at home there and I began to mesh with the atmosphere as he did and develop a stride of my own. Having a medical degree does not make a physician. It is the feel and smell of the hospital surroundings that start the adrenaline flowing and gives one the spiraling thirst for healing. It is learned behavior, ethics, and etiquette. My years working in the Belgian hospitals had prepared me well, but the Harlem family welcomed me and seeing all of those dark, anxious faces with eyes beckoning for recognition and relief from pain touched me so deeply and I spent many hours in the evenings reading charts or just sitting by a bedside to give comfort.

The following spring, I received notification from the Board of Regents that I would be admitted to the medical licensing examination June 25, 1963, and I had spoken with the administrator concerning my position there and it was secure; however, I knew that the next summer, I would have to pass and get board certified or leave. I had diligently set up a routine of study for myself that would afford me time for work, my sorority, and the few remaining friends I had left in the city. In August I had decided that I would participate in the march on Washington. I boarded the bus with a group of friends and I was happy to be part of such a historical moment. It was a very exciting trip for me to have a view of the Lincoln Memorial and a blanket of beautiful colored people on the lawn. When I returned home, I could not stop thinking about the "I have a dream" speech and what it meant to me.

In November, the news of President Kennedy's assassination was aired to the nation. At that very moment, time stood still. I remember thinking how short life is and that I must get it going or I will not reach my goal. He was so young and had so much to give. I was getting old and wanted to do so much still. I called the college to see if my child had heard and how she was faring. She, too, was saddened. She said, "I really wanted to vote for him, Mom, but I was too young. Now I will never get the chance to." I am sure many felt the same, so young, so young, what a tragedy. She called me back a few hours later to tell me that classes had been canceled and there was going to be a memorial service on campus and that some girls were crying openly as they walked to the dorms. I asked if she wished to come home. She said, "not really."

During the Christmas holidays, Butchie brought a friend named Sonja to visit and have dinner with us at the hospital. The young woman lived with her mother in the Bronx and wanted some companionship while in the city. She was a class ahead, but, nevertheless, they got along very well. I knew then that it was time for me to find a domicile and after the New Year, I rented an apartment in the Delano Village so we could have a place to call home—620 Lenox Avenue would be our new address.

Shortly thereafter, I received the news that my brother Emmett died of cardiac arrest. He was only sixty. I immediately called the school and had them send my Butchie home. I had to tell her that her father Emmett had passed away. I didn't know whether to tell her prior to her leaving Greensboro or to wait until her arrival in New York, but I did tell her that we had to travel to Los Angeles as soon as possible. She came in by Greyhound bus and the next morning, we hired a taxi to the airport. During the flight we had a chance to talk about her feelings for her biological parents, both of them, and considering she did not knew either well, she had a deep sense of respect. She had had many long conversations with Emmit when we visited in 1962 and had heard the details of her conception directly from the horse's mouth, so to speak. There wasn't much I could add to that. I also know that she had meshed that knowledge together with what Alice, her biological mother, had told her during her visits to Wilson, North Carolina, where she now lived.

We stayed in California for a week. I had to make sure that all was well with my brother's children and his wife. Not many of us were left of my mother and father's large family, so we took a family portrait to mark the occasion. After that it was time to go back East.

In 1965, I applied for a position at a Jewish Geriatric center in the Bronx—Beth Abraham Home. The Director of Medicine, Dr. Charles Messeloff, took a liking to me right away and we became good friends and great coworkers. Geriatrics was a field that I had never considered, but at this time in my life, I understood the patients more than anyone could know. The surroundings reminded me of the home for the aged that I had visited in Brussels because Europeans have so much respect for their aging parents and go to great lengths to make their final years as comfortable as possible. Most of the patients were Holocaust survivors who had lost everything during the war. Some had arrived to our shores and were reunited with family members and some had migrated and had started over. All of the stories were sad ones, but all of the patients were not sad. They often spoke of how both our people had been in bondage and they seemed to believe that we had so much in common, but I felt not. They came by choice. My forefathers came in chains. Sometimes that angered me, but it did not affect my spirit. The work there was rewarding and I developed a rapport with the staff that helped me practice medicine with ease. I also would see patients at Ralph's office on Lexington Avenue. He had received certification from the state of New York and had set up practice. He seemed to be doing quite well.

It was during that time that my Butchie started dating a young man named Lesley and somehow I knew that he would have a great influence on her life. I remember telling a special coworker, a nurse named Lillie Mae Wheattle, that I thought that he might become my son-in-law someday. The Wheattles were a special family like the Mabry's. They, too, befriended me and the children called me Auntie Hazel. I referred to Lillie Mae as my niece and she became my friend, assistant, and secretary. She was instrumental in arranging my social schedule which included the Zeta Phi Beta meetings, Shaw University Alumni Association, and the Abyssinian Baptist Church all of which were very important to me. Many times we discussed the state boards and my relentless efforts to receive a passing grade. It was her encouragement and constant reassurance that helped me through some of my doubting moments and believe me I had plenty of them.

I had not been using much of my free time for study, nor was I using it wisely. I was engrossed in my work at the home and in my patients at the office. I was using my knowledge and skills, but I would not receive an increase in salary until I was board certified. Butchie was not on scholarship and my savings were greatly diminished and I still owed her a wedding or rather I wanted to give her one if she so desired. She had been a debutante in 1961 and we had saved the gown for that purpose. In the spring of 1966, I made application to take the state boards again, this time with the determination to pass. This was going to be a busy summer, but nothing took precedence over my resolve to be licensed to practice medicine in the state of New York. The week of the examination, I took time off from the job and decided to read rather than cram as I had done on previous occasions such as these. I set up my surroundings to be conducive to review and I was not to be deterred.

This was going to be a busy summer. Butchie had become engaged this past fall and was planning a midsummer wedding. She also was to be graduated with a Bachelors of Arts on June 6 and had already accepted a position in New York with Equitable Life Assurance Society on Avenue of the Americas. I placed an announcement of the upcoming nuptials in the Amsterdam News, a Negro newspaper published in Harlem. I knew that most of my friends past and present were subscribers and would read the article. Friends and relatives helped us as much as they could, considering most of the plans were conducted via long distance calls and the U.S. mail service, but I forged on. I was going to be certified this year, I just knew it.

On June 1, I traveled to North Carolina in preparation for the upcoming graduation ceremonies and to meet Lesley's mother, also to help my daughter pack her numerous belongings, an accumulation of memories of the best years of her life, a personal assumption on my part. After the commencement exercises, the four of us ate a light meal and drove to Fayetteville, North Carolina, to meet with more family members and talk about the wedding. The following Wednesday, Lesley drove us back to Greensboro so we could return to New York and our jobs.

The wedding took place without a hitch, a gorgeous day in July. My little girl looked beautiful and happy and all of our planning came to fruition. After the honeymoon, Butchie went back to her job at Equitable and Lesley worked on his before returning to Greensboro in September to complete his undergraduate studies. Shortly thereafter, Butchie moved to Greensboro as well to be with her husband and once again I was alone.

A week after her departure on September 20, 1966, I received a letter of confirmation from the Board of Regents of the University of the State of New York advising me that I had successfully completed the medical examinations and would be licensed to practice medicine and surgery. I was excited! I was content and overcome with joy. Fourteen years had gone by since I started on this journey and I had come full circle and I was at peace with myself. I felt sorrowful that Mom and Pop could not be here to savor the day, but they were up there somewhere watching me, Little Ethelene from the farm. I called Clara, Poke, and Ronald and I called my little girl who cried and cried.

Now I was truly Dr. Hazel Coley Greene, MD, and nobody could take it away from me. This has been a tough road, I thought to myself, but I finally made it. I had made so many sacrifices for it and God was with me all of the way.

Thank you, Lord, thank you.

From Cotton Fields To Medicine

THE

UNIVERSITY OF THE STATE OF NEW YORK
EDUCATION DEPARTMENT

BE IT KNOWN THAT

Hazel Coley Greene

HAVING GIVEN SATISFACTORY EVIDENCE OF FITNESS AS TO AGE, CHARACTER, PRELIMINARY AND MEDICAL EDUCATION AND ALL OTHER MATTERS REQUIRED BY LAW, WAS EXAMINED AND FOUND DULY QUALIFIED TO RECEIVE THIS

LICENSE TO PRACTISE
MEDICINE AND SURGERY
IN THE STATE OF NEW YORK

New York State Medical License, September 30, 1966

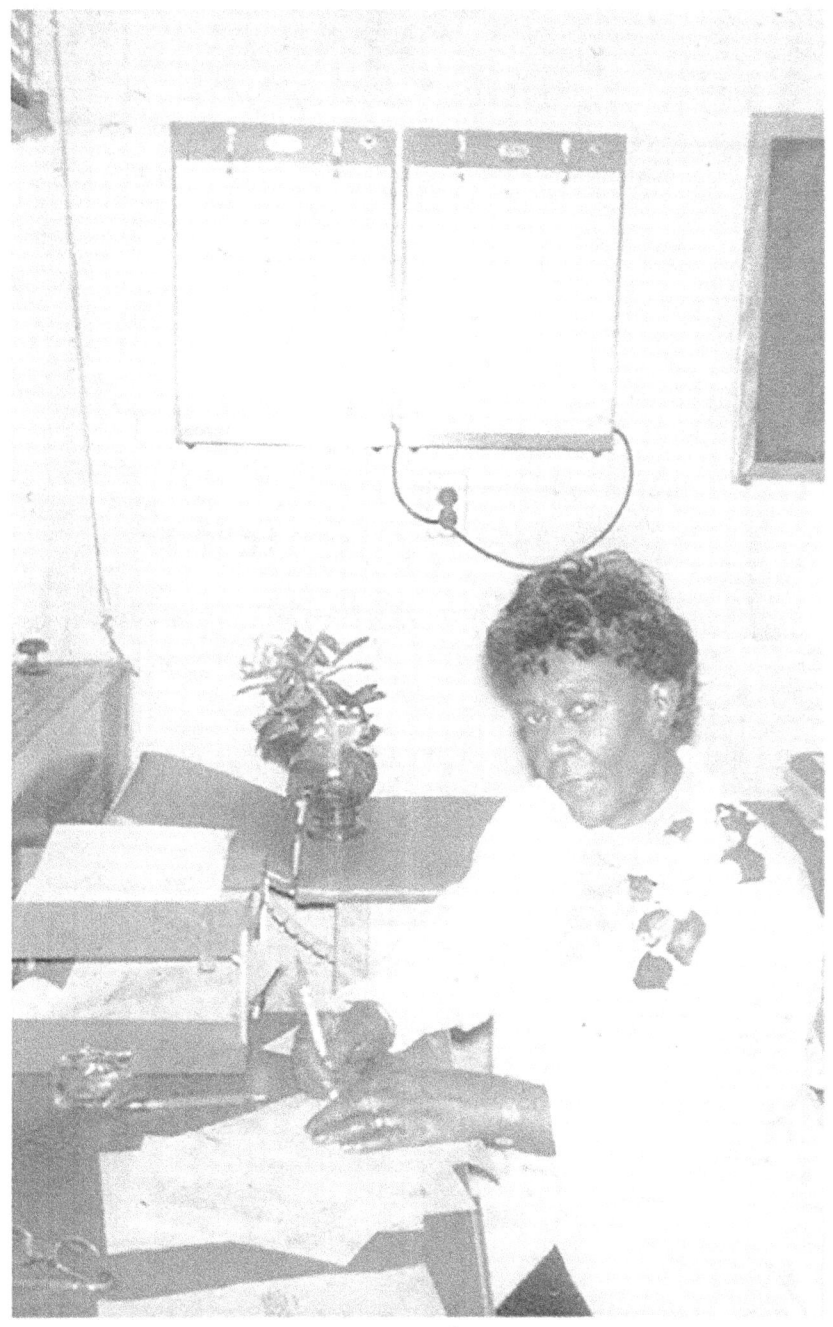

Dr. Greene—Beth Abraham Hospital, 1970

Pacesetters Social Club Acheivement Award, 1978

THE PACESETTERS INC.
1978 ACHIEVEMENT AWARD

Welcome Dr. Hazel Coley-Greene

Good luck and good health to you and
yours for many years to come.

Dr. Hazel Coley-Greene, M.D.

Oh, bring us back once more
the vanished days of yore,
   when the world with faith was filled;
bring back the fervid zeal
the hearts of fire and steel
   the hands that believe and build.

10th ANNUAL EVENING OF ELEGANCE

Epilogue

Dr. Greene maintained a successful practice in medicine as a staff physician at Beth Abraham Hospital until October 1974 when she was stricken by a myocardial infarction and subsequently retired in April 1975 at the age of sixty-seven. In May 1978, she was presented with The Pacesetters Achievement Award for outstanding civic and medical contributions to the Harlem community during a gala evening of elegance in her honor at the Astorian Manor, Queens, New York.

For the next ten years, she traveled the United States, visited the Panama Canal Zone, and returned to Brussels in search of memories of her sojourn in Belgium. After a short illness in 1989, she moved to Atlanta, Georgia to reside with her daughter and family where she remained until her death on August 25, 1996. She was eighty-eight years old.

www.ingramcontent.com/pod-product-compliance
Lightning Source LLC
Chambersburg PA
CBHW072039080526
44578CB00007B/425